Improve Your BRAIN POWER

Dr. G Francis Xavier

PUSTAK MAHAL®

Administrative office and sale centre

J-3/16 , Daryaganj, New Delhi-110002
☎ 23276539, 23272783, 23272784 • *Fax:* 011-23260518
E-mail: info@pustakmahal.com • *Website:* www.pustakmahal.com

Branches
Bengaluru: ☎ 080-22234025 • *Telefax:* 080-22240209
E-mail: pustakmahalblr@gmail.com
Mumbai: ☎ 022-22010941, 022-22053387
E-mail: unicornbooksmumbai@gmail.com
Patna: ☎ 0612-3294193 • *Telefax:* 0612-2302719
E-mail: rapidexptn@gmail.com

This book was earlier published under the title
"Boost Your Brain-Power"

ISBN 978-81-223-0864-8

Edition: 2017

Printed at : **Radha Offset, Delhi**

Dedication

Dedicated with affection and respect to

Most Rev. Dr. Joseph D'Silva

Bishop of Bellary

Acknowledgement

I owe a deep sense of gratitude to all those who have been a source of inspiration and encouragement in my literary pursuit. I present their names in alphabetical order:

Prof. A. Arulmarianathan, V. Acharya, Alvin Chua, Amaladas Fernando, Ms Amudha P. Kandasamy, Anil P. Rao, Ms Anne W. Nderitu, Ashwin Padia, Ayaz Merali, Bro. Jose Thuruthiyal, Bharat Kapasi, Ms Bhavana, Babu K. Varghese, Dave Rogers, R. Devaraj, D. Emmanual Das, Eric Swanson, Francis M. Asiema, P. Gasper, Bro. K.J. George, Gerard Cameons, I. Gunasekar, P.P. Hebbar, L. Henri, Bro. Jose, Mrs Kiran Khullar, Fr Leslie Moras, Mrs & Mr Ilangovan, Ilyas Montri, Luis Kaige, Bro. Jacob Ezhanikatt, I. Joseph Victor, K. Jothiramalingam, Mrs Kalpa Rajesh, R. Kantharaj, M. Kandasami, V.C. Kumaran, O.P. Narang, M. Nellaiappan, Mrs Malathi Gerard, V. Manikesi, M.S. Manjunath, M.B. Meti, P. Narayana Bhat, D.C. Manivannan, Mrs Mary Okela, Sr Nicola Sprenger, Ms Packiam A. Williams, Patrick D'Souza, Dr Pius K. Okela, K. Pon Pandian, Prakash Gangaram, Rajesh K. Padia, Prahalad N. Kalra, J. Ramakrishnan, Reinhard Sprenger, Rajiv Beri, Mrs & Mr E. Ravichandran, Dr S. Rajaram, A.V.K. Ranjith Raj, Dr J.N. Reddy, Roger Khoo, Fr Ronnie Prabhu, S. Sachidanandam, Mrs Selvi Manivannan, Mrs Shaila George, S.G. Sharat Babu, Simon Lourdes Samy, R. Sunder Raj, Sr Taurine, D. Thankaraj, S. Venkataramani.

For over three decades, Most Rev. Dr Joseph D'Silva, Bishop of Bellary, has been my friend, philosopher and guide and this book is dedicated to him.

I wish to immensely thank Dr Thimmappa Hegde, one of India's eminent neurosurgeons, for writing an appropriate Foreword.

I am deeply indebted to my publishers M/s Pustak Mahal and its Editorial Department for producing this book in an excellent manner with immaculate perfection.

My sincere thanks to Arthur Monteiro for editing the typescript.

I am particularly thankful to Nigel Fernandes of Asian Trading Corporation for publishing many of my books and also selling the books published by others.

Last but not the least, my family members, for their patience, support and cooperation: My wife Mrs A Antoniammal, and my children, Dr Denis Xavier, Freeda, Prakash Xavier, Peter and Sheela and grandchildren, Nikita, Alan and Preethika

Foreword

The human brain contains approximately 100 billion neurons or brain cells that are capable of outstanding feats of computation and information processing ability. Unfortunately, most people use no more than 4–10 per cent of the possible potential of their brain.

It is very difficult to understand the operational facets of this enigmatic organ. As a neurosurgeon, I open the skull and repair damaged parts of the brain on a day-to-day basis. From practical experience, I know pretty well how difficult it is to write a book on the complicated subject of brainpower. In this respect, Dr G. Francis Xavier has succeeded remarkably in portraying the anatomy and functioning of the brain in a simple and lucid manner that any layperson can understand comfortably.

It is the brain that makes our life exciting or dull, meaningful or worthless. The brain plays a fantastic and marvellous role in our life and it is our prime duty to take care of this master organ in our body.

Dr Xavier has taken great pains to offer us a variety of techniques to boost our brainpower. All the techniques are simple and practical and can be adopted without much difficulty. His emphasis on the practice of Pranayama and meditation along with proper food and nutrition is quite appropriate to develop super brainpower.

When Dr Xavier approached me to write the Foreword for this wonderful book, I felt extremely delighted because the subject of the brain is so dear to me as a neurosurgeon. It is also an honour and privilege to write a Foreword, as I have had the good fortune of being a student in two of his training programmes: (1) Tap Your Genius – a multi-dimensional personality development programme and the (2) DISH (Develop Integrated Sound Health) programme. Dr Xavier is an effective trainer and is considered a Great Motivator by all participants. He has been a source of great inspiration for me.

I strongly suggest that all those who have a passion to accomplish something great and outstanding in life must go through this book and follow the simple techniques offered to greatly enhance their brain's potential and make their life enchanting.

—Dr Thimmappa Hedge
Head of Department of Neurosurgery
HOSMAT Hospital, Bangalore

Preface

The human brain is the most complex and fascinating organ on this planet. Despite the research done on the brain, there is a lot that we still do not know. But we do know that the potential of the human brain is grossly underutilised. In addition, several myths abound on the functioning of the brain. But the myths are gradually being eradicated, including the biggest one that the functioning of the brain decreases with age.

Worldwide, neuroscientists, psychologists and others interested in human potential have conducted tremendous research on the subject. India and Eastern traditional wisdom from the ages have contributed invaluable insights as well as skills and techniques to greatly enhance brain functioning. **Many of these insights, skills and techniques are presented in this book.** Importantly, they are also effectively imparted at the training programmes *Tap Your Genius* and *Train the Trainers*, which I have been conducting for three decades. Thousands have been trained in India and abroad. These two training programmes effectively blend ancient techniques of the East with modern research findings of the West.

These programmes have enabled executives, professionals and trainers in the field of human resources development (HRD) to enhance their memory power, brain potential, manage time and stress and improve their professional competence. Furthermore, the techniques found in this book are also offered to students, enabling them to score very high marks in exams and also boost their confidence. **This book is an invaluable guide to all who wish to boost their brainpower and thereby attain success and happiness in life.**

Dr G. Francis Xavier
358, 8th Main, Viveknagar
Bangalore – 47, India
Cell: 080–36721820

December 3, 2003

Note to Parents: *Offer this book as a gift to your children. The techniques will not only enhance their brainpower but also help them secure very high marks in exams.*

This book is presented to:

....

Place: Name:

Date: Signature:

Contents

Part One

ANATOMY OF THE BRAIN

A Vital Organ

The most important organ in our body is the brain, and it is also amongst the most neglected. We take great pains by way of physical fitness programmes to preserve our heart. We exercise to strengthen our muscles. But we take our brain for granted. The attention we pay to our heart and lungs does not guarantee that our brain will remain completely functional. We can control and master our environment only if our brain is in proper working order. Even if you want to move your fingers, the command has to come from your brain. All organs, including internal ones like the heart, lungs, liver, etc, function at the dictates of the brain. When a person's leg is paralysed, the problem is not in his legs but in his brain.

Many people who lose limbs like the hands or legs or even parts like the eyes still become successful in their lives provided their brain functions at an optimum level. They simply have to make some minor adjustments. Thanks to advances in medicine we are able to replace the kidneys, lungs and heart with transplants. But the slightest damage to the brain stem, which connects the large brain to the spinal cord, will produce irreversible coma. A person in coma will continue to live with all the other organs functioning normally, except consciousness. But he would only vegetate – leading a life without any meaning. The brain is the only organ that we cannot live without. The joy and sorrow of life comes from the brain. We operate our entire life through the functioning of the brain. The structure and functioning of the brain is so intricate and complicated that it can never be replaced with a transplant.

Without the brain functioning properly, life is not worth living. Our aim in life is not just physical survival. Just think of those who are insane or suffer from Alzheimer's disease that completely takes away memory. They only exist physically. Only the brain has the capacity to control and shape the environment around us. The extent of control that we can exercise depends upon the mental abilities that we have developed in our brain over a lifetime.

It is generally believed that as we advance in age brainpower declines. Many ask: "Will I lose brainpower and become forgetful just because I am growing old?" The answer is an emphatic 'No'. Loss of brainpower as we advance in age is not inevitable. Several research results have recently proved that the power of the brain can be maintained throughout life, and can also be improved. We have to take preventive steps early in life to be able to keep up the tempo and power of our brain, as we grow older. This book seeks to present the **techniques to develop super brainpower**.

Physical Aspects of the Brain

The brain is safely secured in your head. It should not be confused with the mind. The **brain is physical**; the **mind is functional**. The brain is the **hardware**, the **mind** is the **software**. There are approximately 100 billion neurons in the brain. The adult brain weighs about 1.4 kg and is only 2 per cent of the body weight.

The brain has **three major parts**: the brain stem, cerebellum, and cerebrum.

The **brain stem** sits atop your spinal column. This is the first part of the brain to be formed in the womb. It has three nerve centres – the midbrain, pons and medulla oblongata. The nerve centres in the midbrain help control movements of the eye. The pons links the two hemispheres of the cerebrum. The medulla regulates breathing, heartbeat and blood flow. In short, the brain stem takes care of the **survival mechanism** of the body.

The **cerebellum** is located just behind the brain stem and manages the movement of our body. Therefore, it contains

memory for movement. This is called kinaesthetic memory or muscle memory. Most good **athletes** have very well developed cerebellums.

The **cerebrum** is the final stage of brain development in evolution. This is the real brain where **thinking and feelings** arise. The cerebrum is divided into four areas or lobes: (a) the **frontal lobe** deals with abstract problem solving, (b) the **parietal lobe** helps process information from the senses, (c) the **occipital lobe** governs vision, and (d) the **temporal lobe** controls memory, hearing and language.

The cerebrum contains the **neocortex** and the **limbic system**. These two work in tandem. The neocortex is the **thinking brain** and the limbic system is the **feeling brain**. The limbic system is where the mind meets the body and the endocrine system interfaces with the brain. It is also where thought meets emotions. When the physical health of the limbic system is stimulated, one can effectively operate the intellectual and emotional aspects of life.

The primary parts of the **limbic system** are the hippocampus, the amygdala, the hypothalamus, the thalamus and the pituitary glands.

(a) **Hippocampus** stores dry and unemotional facts of short-term memories. It ships most long-term memories to the neocortex.

(b) **Amygdala** stores emotional memories. When there is an emotional impact in a thought, it is automatically shifted to long-term memory. Therefore, **emotion plays a crucial role in long-term memory**. In other words, any experience involved with strong emotions is not forgotten for a long time.

(c) **Hypothalamus** is closely connected to the amygdala. Its primary function is to tell the body how to respond to various situations. Based on the situation it gives messages to the pituitary gland. This is the master gland in the body that relays the message to the rest of the body. The messages are sent through hormones. The hypothalamus controls body temperature, hunger and sexual functions. In a crisis, it sends out orders for more adrenaline.

(d) **Thalamus** picks up all incoming sensory messages except smell, and relays them to the appropriate processing centre in the brain. It is basically a relay station.

(e) **Pituitary** is the master endocrine gland and gives orders to other glands about what to do. It receives messages from the hypothalamus and helps the body produce hormones it needs to respond to various situations. This is considered as the **third eye**, involved in intuition.

The **brain generates electricity**. The brain cells run on electricity and the brain has enough electricity to light a 25-watt bulb. Thoughts travel through brain cells on electrical currents. Long strings of brain cells light up with electrical energy to form complete thoughts and emotions.

Most **brain cells** are elongated, shaped rather like trees with a branch system. The roots of the neuron (brain cell) are called **axons**. Information flows into axons from the dentric branches of adjacent neurons. Information travels to the axons of another neuron in the form of an electrical impulse. Eventually, this forms a complete chain like thought or memory. New dentric branches can be stimulated to grow.

Brain Research

The biological architecture of the brain was not known till recently. The brain was simply not accessible for research as it is buried in a relatively impenetrable box, the skull.

In 1972, **Computerised Tomography (CT) Scan** and later **Positron Emission Tomography (PET) Scan** were invented. They could turn out clear images of **brain anatomy and metabolism** and track chemicals as they made their way through elaborate pathways in the brain. After the introduction of the scan devices, we are able to understand with remarkable detail the structure of our brain and how it works. It is possible to study the living brain through the CT scan and PET scan.

It is amazing to observe the changes that take place in the brain when it is thinking, feeling, processing information, registering memory, etc. Sophisticated colourful 3-D brain images can trace the routes of neurotransmitters as they congregate to elicit mood changes and lay down long-term memory. Scientists are now able to physically see the amount of blood flow to various parts of the brain and also how much energy the brain uses for its various functions.

It has been ascertained that **older people** have to **work harder** than youngsters to process or retrieve the same information.

Scientists can map brain activity in response to music – whether you hear a pleasing melody or discordant notes. The latest additions include functional **MRI (Magnetic Resonance Imaging)** and **SPECT (Single Photon Emission Computerised Tomography)**. They can track the working of a living human brain to the minutest level.

Right Brain and Left Brain

The three-part brain is also divided into a right and left hemisphere. Each hemisphere is responsible for different modes of thinking, each specialising in certain skills.

Although there is some crossover and interaction between the two sides, the thinking processes of the **left brain** are: (a) logical (b) linear (c) orderly (d) rational (e) sequential (f) organised (g) systematic (h) reality based (i) dealing with abstract ideas (j) verbal expression (k) reading (l) writing (m) auditory association (n) identifying facts and figures (o) phonetics and symbolism and (p) **micro approach**.

The **right brain** thinking modes are: (a) creative (b) imaginative (c) random (d) intuitive (e) non-verbal ways of knowing (f) unorganised (g) spatial awareness (h) shape and pattern recognition (i) art (j) music (k) colour sensitivity

(l) feeling the presence of objects and people (m) visualisation and (n) **macro approach**.

To lead an effective life both hemispheres of the brain should be given **equal importance**. Those who make use of both hemispheres of the brain tend to produce better results in life. They learn very fast. Most geniuses use both left and right brains. Unfortunately, the modern system of education emphasises left-brain activities and neglects right-brain activities.

Brain Wave Frequency

The brain emits faint electrical impulses in the form of mental waves. These waves can be measured in microvolts by an electroencephalograph (EEG). There is a close relationship between the frequency, voltage and amplitude of brain waves and the mental state of an individual according to his consciousness. These waves represent a manifestation of certain **internal psychological states of the mind** associated with the corresponding activities of the brain. Decades of scientific investigation of the brain's electrical activity have proved that alterations in the EEG represent changes in thoughts and perceptions. When these electrical waves change, either in frequency or in amplitude, our state of mind changes too: one pattern of waves for doing arithmetic, for instance, and another very different one for daydreaming.

The four types of brain waves are: (a) beta waves (b) alpha waves (c) theta waves and (d) delta waves.

(a) **Beta Waves:** In a wide-awake person beta waves are emitted from the brain with frequencies **over 14 cycles per second**. These waves are present when the active thinking mind is turned towards the **outside world**. When one is stressed or tense the brain emits high frequencies of beta waves.

(b) **Alpha Waves:** When there is relaxed awareness with a move towards interiority, alpha waves appear with frequencies of **7 to 13 cycles per second**. Alpha waves represent a **relaxed state of mind**, passivity and a non-anxious and tensionless state.

(c) **Theta Waves:** When consciousness is blurred in drowsiness, or when one slips towards unconsciousness or during disturbed sleep, theta waves appear with frequencies of **4 to 7 cycles per second**. Research studies found that in **children** up to the age of about nine the most commonly produced frequency is theta. It was also found that in a heightened form of **meditation** or while creatively engaged, theta waves appear. This may prove that when negative emotions are completely absent theta waves are present. In the absence of negative emotions one is relaxed. Therefore, it may be safely concluded that **emotions play a tremendous role** in producing this pattern of mental waves. If one is able to think and behave in a childlike manner he can easily produce theta waves at any point of time.

(d) **Delta Waves:** In the absence of consciousness, as in sound **dreamless sleep**, delta waves appear in the EEG, with frequencies **below 4 cycles** per second.

When the brain waves reach zero point, the brain is dead. To be productive, it is better that the brain emits alpha waves most of the time in our wakeful state.

✡✡✡

Old Myths and New Discoveries

Any discovery related to the brain means that we are discovering something new about ourselves. Recent research into the brain has exploded many long-held beliefs.

Size and Weight

It used to be thought that heredity determines the size and weight of the brain, that it is a fixed entity and nothing can be done to change it. Now research has proved that the size and weight of the brain can be increased through **external stimulation** and **enriched environment**.

Impact of Ageing

It was believed that after reaching maturity the growth of the brain stopped completely. It was also believed that there is a continuous loss of brain cells as we advance in age, resulting in decreased intelligence and creativity among the elderly. Now studies have shown that with proper stimulation the **brain can continue to grow**, producing enhanced intelligence and better functioning even at the ripe old age of 90 years.

Regeneration of Brain Cells

Neuroscientists firmly believed that the brain cells in the body proliferate only till the age of two and then the growth of brain cells completely stopped. It was also believed that the loss of brain cells took place continuously in a person's lifetime. Now many studies have shown that neurons can regenerate and the **lost cells can be replaced** under the right conditions and stimulation, in much the same way as our skin can heal itself after it is cut.

The Two Hemispheres

It was earlier thought that depending upon the type of task at hand, either the left or the right hemisphere would be in operation. As the tasks changed the dominance of the side would also change. This suggested that we could use only one side of the brain at a time. But now it is clear that while a person is in **deep meditation** or **intense creativity**, both hemispheres begin to produce the same type of brain waves in a single, coherent rhythm, operating in unison. This is called **brain synchronisation**. It has recently become clear that certain brain stimulation devices can rapidly boost the brain into this beneficial state.

Influence of Lights and Sounds

There was a belief that any conceivable mental state is created by the interaction of electrical and chemical activity in the brain and that we have absolutely no control over our mental state. But recent research reveals that it is **possible to create any kind of mental state** like euphoria, reverie, recall of past experiences, sexual excitement, deep concentration and heightened creativity by triggering specific areas in the brain through mechanical devices that use sounds, lights and electromagnetic fields. It is now confirmed that through external stimuli brain activities can be altered and shaped.

Control of Thoughts, Emotions and Moods

It was firmly believed that the activities of the brain, such as its rhythm through electrical activity and secretion of brain chemicals, are beyond our conscious control. But after the introduction of **biofeedback machines** it is now possible to **bring** the involuntary systems such as our blood pressure, heart rate and secretion of hormones **under conscious control**. Many sophisticated and sensitive machines have come into the market, which can monitor and give us feedback on what are generally considered mental states. By sensing the brain's electrical activity and simultaneously "relaying" that activity to us in easily understood images, these machines enable users to observe their brain states and change them. In effect, you can learn to alter and control your own thoughts, emotions, moods and mental states, at will.

Enormous Potential

In the past the actual potential of the brain was not recognised. Recent studies indicate that the human brain is capable of far greater feats of learning, remembering, and creating than had previously been imagined. Under proper conditions, normal humans can **absorb, store, process, and recall vast amounts of information**.

✡✡✡

Unique Features of the Brain

A Physical Organ

The brain is basically a physical organ composed of flesh and blood. Its functions such as thinking, feeling, registering facts and figures and reproducing them (memory) are completely physical in nature. Therefore, **a thought** or **an emotion** in the brain exists as a **physical entity**. If we have a very powerful microscope, we can physically "see" the thought or the emotion embedded in our brain cells.

As the brain is a physical organ, it is vulnerable to **damage** through physical substances like **alcohol, tobacco and mind-altering drugs**. The brain can also be damaged through **stress** and tension, poor nutrition, lack of physical and mental exercise and various **toxic substances**. However, the brain can also be protected from such physical abuses and its power can be enhanced through a variety of physical and biochemical approaches. By adopting certain methods it is **possible to physically change poor memory into a good one**. In this sense, mind and memory can also be considered physical entities. It is quite possible now to intervene in the mind and memory on a physical level.

Electrically Powered and Electricity-generating Organ

The brain has an estimated 100 billion neurons. Each **neuron** in itself is a computer, producing and transmitting electrical impulses. Since each neuron can be connected with thousands of other neurons, each simultaneously **sending and receiving electrical impulses** to and from thousands of other neurons, a single signal from one neuron can quickly reach and electrically alter millions of other neurons. Since each of these millions of neurons is unique, displaying slightly different response patterns from the others, the brain is an unimaginably complex electrical network, with billions of electromagnetic impulses flying in all directions every second.

According to the National Academy of Sciences, USA, a single human brain has a greater number of possible connections among its nerve cells than the total number of atomic particles in the universe.

Unlimited Potential

The brain is an unbelievably intricate entity in the universe. Even the most sophisticated computer in the world cannot have the **storage capacity** and information processing ability of the brain of an ordinary person. Unfortunately, no one utilises the full capacity of the brain. Even **geniuses have used only a fraction** of their brain capacity. Everyone uses his or her brain but no one has tapped its full potential.

Ability of Recall

The **temporal lobe** of the brain holds the long-term memory. If an electrode is placed on this lobe, one can easily recall past experiences with perfect accuracy. Even if you think that your **memory** is poor, you can definitely **improve its potential** and develop a sharp memory.

Damage by Stress

When a person endures stress on a regular basis, he profusely secretes the brain-destroying chemical, **cortisol**. This **diminishes brainpower**. Long-term chronic stress hormones are bad for the brain. Recent research reveals that persistent stress can actually alter the very structure and functioning of the brain cells. **Stress causes brain damage.** Short-lived stress may be good for brain functioning. The stress of taking a test, for example, can stimulate a burst of adrenaline that improves memory. But long-lasting inappropriate stress triggered by everyday events, such as work frustration, traffic jams and financial worries can wear your brain down, eroding important neuronal connections, eventually bringing on forgetfulness. Research suggests that **chronic stress** can actually **shrink the hippocampus**, the memory centre of the brain. If you want to improve your brainpower, learn to manage your stress effectively and develop a sense of happiness and quietude.

Plasticity

Many research studies have proved the brain's awesome "plasticity" – it has the stunning ability to continually reinvent itself. Any damage caused to the brain need not, therefore, be permanent. The brain can **grow new cells** and more thinking power can be obtained out of the existing cells. When the biological environment is conducive new cells are likely to grow. It is possible to accelerate the functioning of the brain by improving the existing brain cells. All brain cells have branches or dendrites that reach out and connect with other brain cells. Thoughts travel through these connections. **The more connections, the better your brain works.** The brain can change its structure, grow more synapses, sprout more dendrites, and increase its neuronal connectivity. A single neuron can have 100,000 synapses that connect it with neighbouring brain cells. There are probably trillions of interconnections made possible by your dendrites and axons.

Recent studies prove that **new connections** can be formed at virtually **any age**. One of the simplest ways to form new connections is simply **to think**. Many people don't think. Thinking is not recollecting the past or projecting into the future. It is to **live in the present**. If you develop the habit of living in the present you have an enormous potential to boost your brainpower. Its plasticity provides a wider scope to improve the potential of the brain at any age. It is **never too late to regenerate your brain**.

A Mystical Entity

In spite of numerous studies on the brain much about it remains a mystery. Even today no one can say with authority how memory is formed. Many functions of the brain are not completely understood. Even with the latest developments in laser technology and the miracle of microchips, the brain largely remains **an enigmatic organ**. Its functions still remain a mystery. We do not know with certainty whether brain and intelligence are one and the same. Can we say with authority that the brain is merely a physical organ while intelligence is something intangible? Is it possible for scientists to fathom the properties of intelligence with greater detail?

Neuroscientists and psychologists are still debating about the role played by **heredity and environment** for the development of intelligence. How is it that children of the same parents display different aptitudes and talents? In my own case, my eldest son has become a doctor, the second boy a computer engineer and my daughter is an English lecturer. Are our very personalities and natures only the by-products of chemical neurotransmissions and electrical connections going on in a mass of pinkish-grey organic matter?

These secrets and others are still locked within the 1.4 kg organ inside your skull, the brain. But one thing is certain: **by physically improving your brain, you can easily improve its functioning**.

Use It or Lose It

The brain should be **constantly used** or else it loses its power. When the brain is stimulated intellectually and physically you can see the measurable changes in its structure. The way you use your brain can alter its very form. Such activity can prod the brain to **produce new connections** between neurons and even create brand new brain cells.

The brain is like a muscle – using it makes it grow and expand; disuse causes it to atrophy. Thus, education makes the brain more resistant to deterioration and disease, because people who earn degrees tend to exercise their brains more, building a more lively, resilient and complex brain. It is commonly found that **well-educated persons live longer**, retaining better mental and physical abilities than less educated persons. Also, **less educated persons suffer more from Alzheimer's** than well-educated persons. Memory deterio-ration and dementia occur rarely among educated persons.

Novelty and Exercise

We have earlier seen that the brain stem deals with the survival mechanism. The brain stem has an area called **reticular formation**. It is wired to respond selectively to the new and exotic. New challenges activate reticular formation and stimulate the growth of dendrites. Therefore, it is strongly recommended that **to retain the brain's potential**, one should not only remain active but also **take up new pursuits** every now and then.

Exercise increases blood flow to the brain. Research indicates that older humans who exercise score higher on tests of cognitive function than non-exercisers. **Exercise** infuses **new life** into the brain.

Genetic Influence

The innate potential of the brain differs from person to person. Genetic and prenatal influences do play a role in developing brainpower. But recent studies have shown that **genes alone do not determine a person's destiny**. Other environmental factors – including diet, education and lifestyle – are also powerful determinants of mental functioning.

"The genes are the bricks and mortar to build a brain. The environment is the architect," says Christine Hohmann. It is estimated that about 30 per cent of the characteristics of ageing are genetically based, while the environment influences the balance 70 per cent. People are largely responsible for their own brainpower and ageing process.

Free Radicals the Primary Enemy

As we advance in age, natural **wear and tear** occurs in the brain. When the body burns oxygen to make energy for cells, by-products called **free radicals** are thrown off. They are also produced when the body is deprived of oxygen, or when it is exposed to sunlight, X-rays, tobacco smoke, vehicular exhaust and various environmental pollutants. These free radicals damage DNA, change the biochemical mix in the body, wear down cell membranes and sometimes actually **kill cells**. This degeneration probably occurs as a result of long-term exposure to free radicals and ultimately causes a long list of diseases and ailments, including **memory loss**.

Under ideal conditions, free radicals are kept in check by **antioxidants** released by the cells of the immune system or by natural antioxidant substances found in the bloodstream, certain foods you eat, and the liver. A problem occurs when too many free radicals are generated and overload the body's scavenging mechanism. Over the years free radical damage accumulates in the cells and their energy production slows down. In nerve cells, attacks by free radicals cause dendrites to retract and synapses to vanish, dramatically cutting back on a cell's communication abilities. Eventually, free radical damage **threatens neuronal survival**. The longer you live, the more free radicals your cells generate, making you more susceptible to simple age-related brain damage as well as degenerative brain disorders like Alzheimer's disease.

Some brains age much faster than others due to excessive free-radical damage, much of it being needless and **preventable**. The best way to avoid and even reverse this age-induced brain deficit is to **get more antioxidants** into your brain to neutralise the destructive free radicals. Such antioxidants rush to a free radical and destroy it. This strategy has produced thrilling results, identifying antioxidants as one of the most promising ways to save your brain.

Brain Activity is Essentially Chemical

The signals received from the various senses cause chemical reactions in the brain. Such reactions trigger further actions in various parts of the brain. Neurotransmitters are **chemical messengers** responsible for the transfer of information, memory and mood. If your telephone lines do not work you cannot talk to your friend. Similarly, if neurotransmitters are malfunctioning, information cannot be transferred and retained.

Master Control Centre

The brain is the master control centre of your whole body. It consumes 25 per cent of all metabolic energy. It stimulates motor functions, digestion, growth and tissue repair. It interprets your sensory experience and decides which physical and emotional responses to make. Despite this incredible power, your brain constitutes only two per cent of your body's weight. This makes it highly sensitive. **Nutritional deficiencies** can cause brain imbalances that send shock waves through your entire body, resulting in everything from fatigue and forgetfulness to depression and anxiety.

Nutrients

By maximising the health and functioning of the neuron, we maximise the basic building block of mental performance and intelligence. Nutrients strongly **influence mental functioning**. Several "smart pills" work by increasing the level of the neurotransmitters, the "chemical messengers" the brain cells use to communicate with each other. More information on smart pills is given in Part Two of the book.

Chronological and Biological Ageing

Chronological ageing is different from **biological ageing**. Chronological ageing is simply the measurement of the **passage of time**. We will continue to have birthdays; the pages of the calendar will continue to turn. **Biological ageing**

is the gradual destruction of the human body. Most people believe that biological and chronological ageing happen simultaneously. This is a myth.

As we grow older with time, we do not have to destroy our bodies. In fact, we now know that **biological ageing** can be **slowed down**, stopped and, in some cases, **even reversed**.

Psychosomatic Diseases Originate in the Brain

Your brain does not hibernate in isolation within the skull. It **communicates with all other parts of your body** through the nerve pathways that go down the spinal cord to your muscles and internal organs. Activities that occur in your brain can conceivably affect every single cell in your body, directly or indirectly. This is because of the extensive nerve network lacing throughout your body tissues. Even your blood vessels dilate and constrict in response to the steady stream of pulse signals originating in the lower centres of your brain. Of course, your brain receives an enormous number of pulses every second from the many sensor nerves that originate in the tissue of your muscles and organs. This is how your brain makes sense of what is happening all over your body and responds with the necessary regulatory signals. This interactive relationship between your brain and the other parts of the body also forms the basis for psychosomatic disease and psychosomatic wellness.

Multiple Intelligence

Gardner Murphy spent 15 years in research on the brain and developed a theory that each person has seven kinds of intelligence, all different and equally important. These are:

(1) **Linguistic** – the ability to deal with any language and use appropriate words to express ideas and concepts clearly and fluently. Poets and writers come under this category.

(2) **Logical** – the ability to understand numerical relationship – talents in solving mathematical problems, science, statistics and logic. Scientists and mathematicians have logical intelligence.

(3) **Artistic** – also called spatial intelligence – the ability to think in pictures and images and to transform the visual-spatial world. Artists, engineers, sculptors, designers, architects, *et al.* fall in this category.

(4) **Musical** – the ability to hear and produce rhythms, melodies and harmonies. People dealing with sound, such as musicians, playback singers, music directors, *et al.* have more of this intelligence

(5) **Bodily or Kinaesthetic** – athletic intelligence to control one's body with dexterity. Well-known sports personalities have kinaesthetic intelligence in abundance.

(6) **Interpersonal** – the ability to understand and interact with other people. Politicians, executives, social workers, *et al.* have it in good measure.

(7) **Intra-personal** – intelligence of the inner self – people who are able to control their emotions and passions and those dealing with reflection, contemplation and meditation. Saints, seers and yogis have this.

One of the ways to measure brainpower is through standard IQ (Intelligent Quotient) tests. In the light of the theory of multiple intelligence, it is proved that **IQ tests cannot measure** very much of our **brainpower**. It may perhaps measure only one or two of the seven kinds of intelligence.

It is now assumed that there might be seven different and relatively independent brain systems, corresponding to each of these multiple intelligences. Of late, scientists confirm that **linguistic and logical** intelligences are seated in the **left brain** and the **rest in the right brain**. Unfortunately, in schools and colleges students are encouraged to develop only the left-brain activities, neglecting the right-brain activities.

✡✡✡

How Memory is Stored and Retrieved

Information is registered in the brain in three ways: from **seeing**, **hearing** and **doing**. From these follow **visual** memory, **auditory** memory and **kinaesthetic** memory.

Most **auditory** memories are stored in the **left side** of the brain's neocortex and **visual** memories in the **right side** of the neocortex. **Kinaesthetic** memories, by and large, are stored in the **cerebellum**. Most people are relatively adept at laying down one of the three types of memory than the other two.

The general trend is that memory constitutes 65% visual, 20% auditory and 15% kinaesthetic. When a memory is encoded visually, auditorily and kinaesthetically, it will exist in a maximum number of brain cells. Good teachers often try to tailor their lessons to the learning style preferred by each of their students.

Visual learners learn more quickly than auditory and kinaesthetic learners. **Kinaesthetic** learning is not very effective for most type of academic subjects, but it is by far the most **enduring** type of memory. Kinaesthetic memory endures well partly because the cerebellum (where most kinaesthetic memory resides) is relatively less vulnerable to degenerative damage than the neocortex and the hippocampus, which process most visual and auditory learning. Once you learn to type or drive a car, you never forget how. Kinaesthetic memory also seems to be the only form of memory that functions best without the help of associated memories from other parts of the brain. The more you think about a skill memory, such as playing tennis or cricket, the less you are able to do it. That is why athletes playing in games simply go with the flow of their muscle memory.

The primary area of the brain that ships short-term memories to long-term storage is the limbic system, particularly of the hippocampus and amygdala. The limbic system is the emotional brain, and one of its major jobs is to decide whether a memory is worth keeping. Memories are shipped to long-term storage by the limbic system in two basic ways. One way occurs when your emotional limbic system becomes excited or stimulated about an event or a fact. When this happens you naturally secrete excitatory catecholamine neurotransmitters, such as norepinephrine, that powerfully engrave memories upon the brain.

The other primary way that you send messages to long-term storage is by repeating them to yourself. Even the most boring facts can be memorised through repetition. One important biological mechanism that supports learning by repetition is called **long-term potentiation**, discovered in 1973. This phenomenon is great news for anyone who wants to biologically develop a good memory. Because of long-term potentiation or LTP, every time you see or think about a particular piece of information, it becomes biologically easier to remember it the next time you are exposed to it. Each exposure doesn't just add to your memory, it adds exponentially.

In other words, if you see the same information five times, you will be more likely to remember it not five times, but about twenty times. This happens because the memory trace that was created by the information becomes, in effect, an often-travelled road. The path of the memory is, so to speak, beaten down, making the path easier for neurotransmitters to travel.

✡✡✡

Part Two

POWERFUL TECHNIQUES TO DEVELOP SUPER BRAINPOWER

Developing Super Brainpower

This book aims to offer you a variety of techniques to boost your brainpower into Super Brainpower. The listing includes the things that you **should do** and the things you **should avoid**. For easy reference, they are listed **alphabetically**.

Attitude

Brainpower can be improved through a variety of techniques at any age. Mental power is not a fixed entity. **Believe** that you can gain more brainpower. A positive attitude comes from strong faith in yourself and your capabilities. How your brain ages is directly related to the way you view your life. If you are happy and view life positively, your brain will be young and healthy.

Affirmation

To develop a positive attitude one should practise the technique of affirmation. By affirmation we mean the **repetition** of certain positive statements to ourselves. One who wants to develop super brainpower may repeat to himself any one of the following statements:

- My brainpower is improving day by day.
- Learning and remembering are easy for me.
- My mind works effectively and efficiently.
- My memory is powerful and my mind is alert.

You can create your own statement and repeat it often. The statement that you repeat will be submerged in your subconscious mind and programme you to use your brain to the fullest extent.

Alcohol

It is generally believed that a low intake of alcohol will increase the excitability of neurons and give a quick flush of energy. But studies now show that alcohol is a **neurotoxic** agent even at lower doses. If you think a drink or two enhances your experience of the world, you are deluded. Alcohol actually slows down reaction time to visual and auditory stimuli. It **dulls the senses** so that people who drink find it harder to discriminate between light intensities and sounds. It is a **"make-you-stupid" drug**. It is the most potent and most toxic of the legal psychoactive drugs. The first area to be affected by alcohol is the limbic system or emotional area of the brain. Chronic alcohol abuse can produce **memory loss** in many ways.

Antioxidants

Free radicals are harmful to the body and brain. An antioxidant is a natural substance that acts as a free-radical scavenger, literally consuming them within the cells of your body. Minimise sources of free-radical contamination from your diet and lifestyle and optimise the consumption of antioxidants, which include nutrients such as **vitamins B1, B5, B6, C and E, ginseng, gingko biloba, zinc and selenium**. Selenium works in combination with vitamin E. Vitamin C is a major antioxidant. (*See also under Free Radicals.*)

Aromatherapy

Smells and aromas can instantly affect your mind, triggering joy or disgust. Since the sensitivity to aroma differs from person to person, the choice of the type of aroma conducive for stimulating your brain is a subjective matter. For example, lavender relaxes the brain and helps it function better.

Awareness

Attention may be another word for awareness. Normally, our mind flits around like a mischievous monkey. To be attentive requires an effort. The three major functions of the brain are thinking, feeling and action. The brain is tremendously stimulated when you are **aware of your thoughts, feelings and actions**. If you are aware of your action the moment you do it, this same energy imprint remains later, even years later, to enable you to remember it. The more you pay attention to the events that occur in the present time, the easier you can recall these events, as memories, in the future.

Further, this exercise of paying attention (awareness) to the present moment builds concentration, focus, mindfulness, alertness, and the skill of processing and storing information that becomes memory.

Biorhythm Cycles

Our body has three constituent elements – physical, emotional and intellectual. They operate cyclically. The universe itself is a cyclic operation based on different forms of energy. The human body is a creation of Nature made up of three types of energy – physical energy, emotional energy and intellectual energy.

These innate energies begin operating in our life the moment we are born. They represent the ebb and flow of energy in our body. They operate in a cyclical rise and fall. They are called **biorhythm cycles**. Biorhythm cycles have tremendous influence on our life. The **physical** cycle takes **23 days** to complete; the **emotional** cycle takes **28 days**; and the **intellectual 33 days**.

The intellectual cycle regulates intellectual faculties like memory, alertness, receptivity to ideas, understanding, logical and analytical thinking, creativity, imagination, etc. It lasts for 33 days – 16.5 days positive and 16.5 days negative. During the positive phase the mind is open to new ideas. Memory is at its best, which includes both the retentive and recall faculties. You are able to put together different ideas and come to a good understanding. The logical as well as the creative thinking processes are at their peak. The ability to tackle a new situation with quick understanding is at its best in this period. During the negative phase the intellectual energy is low, though it does not mean that people become stupid or dull during this period. Mental fatigue is more frequent.

Calculating Biorhythm: Add up all the days you have lived since birth and divide the resulting number by the length of each cycle (23, 28 and 33). Remember to take into account leap years. The remainder will give the point at which the current biorhythm cycle is. For example, if it is 33,010 days since your birth, you have completed 1,000 intellectual cycles and are into the 10th day of the current cycle. This will be a positive phase. From here it is easy to interpret. By maintaining a proper record of biorhythm cycles you avoid the trouble of calculating them frequently. There are now devices to instantly calculate biorhythm cycles by feeding the date of birth in your computer. Biorhythm software is also available in the market.

Blood Pressure

Chronic blood pressure (which involves a thickening of the cerebral arteries) cuts down the normal flow of oxygen into your brain. People with diastolic readings of 90 and above start showing significant decline in general memory, mental tasks involving short-term memory and the fluidity or flexibility of intelligence. Therefore, steps should be taken to avoid or control blood pressure.

Brainex

This consists of several exercises designed to stimulate the brain. These exercises are given in Part Three of this book.

Brainstorming

The objective of brainstorming is to collect as many ideas as possible without any hesitation and inhibition. All ideas are allowed a chance. Even the most ridiculous, frivolous and outright dumb ideas are welcome. This would ensure that contributors are not inhibited by the fear that they might say something stupid. The essential aspect here is that the growing list of ideas would help trigger new and better ones. In a brainstorming session the brain functions rapidly and effectively to produce as many ideas as possible.

Breastfeeding

Dr Minear, an instructor in paediatrics at Harvard Medical School, USA, stresses the enormous value of breastfeeding for a child's mental development. It serves as both good nutrition and an excellent psychological bond between mother and infant. He suggests that breastfeeding should continue for at least four to six months and up to a year or two. Mother's milk is the single best brain food we know.

Biofeedback

The brain functions very effectively when it produces alpha waves. Meditation enables one to reach alpha waves of mental state. Some find meditation difficult, as it demands self-discipline. Biofeedback can help them. Biofeedback is a mechanical device for presenting information externally about what is happening internally. It presents our state of consciousness openly so that we can have an objective insight into the state of our mind. Biofeedback is done by equipping the electroencephalograph (EEG) with instruments that indicate with sounds and flashing lights that the person studying his brain at work is now producing alpha, theta or other brain waves. He can gradually train himself to enter an internal state of consciousness of his choice by observing these lights and sounds. Biofeedback machines enable one to reach alpha waves of mental state at one's volition. This in turn would enhance brainpower.

Calmness

The brain functions most effectively when calm. When negative emotions like anger, irritation, animosity, hatred, etc are present the blood flows to the entire body at a heightened level. For concentrated thought the blood flow should be focused more to the area of the brain. Therefore, negative emotions obstruct powerful concentration.

Choline

A study done by Dr Nataraj and co-workers at the National Institute of Health, United States, showed that a dietary supplement of 10 grams of choline a day did have an obvious effect on some components of memory in a scientifically controlled study in normal subjects.

Choline is the substance from which the brain makes acetylcholine, a neurotransmitter involved in memory function. It also helps the structural integrity of the synapses, which are the points of communication between brain cells. As we advance in age choline levels drop sharply.

Clogged Intestine

If you are chronically constipated or internally sluggish, your brain also becomes sluggish. Constipation brings down energy level. This in turn lowers the effective functioning of the brain. Stagnant bowels produce lassitude, fatigue, irritability, restlessness, intolerance and frequent illnesses.

Concentration

Concentration alone could double your brainpower. You can't do two things at once – at least not well. When you split your attention, you cut your potential brainpower in half. Only if you have a healthy brain can you concentrate well. Concentration is also a result of will power. When you make an effort to concentrate your brain is stimulated.

Creeping and Crawling

Before walking upright the child has to creep and crawl around the house. Creeping and crawling forges a working relationship between the midbrain, eyes and hands. It helps reknit your sensory motor experience. This in turn would restimulate your midbrain. This may seem a ridiculous way to gain brainpower, but it works.

Diets for the Brain

Food plays a major role in boosting brainpower. For best results, note the following points:

(a) Eat only when hungry.

(b) Eat a low-fat diet – fat-laden blood does not circulate well.

(c) Make fruits and vegetables the major part of your diet.

(d) Your brain's only fuel is glucose.

(e) When your blood sugar is low, your brain functions poorly.

(f) When you go on a starvation diet, you starve your brain too.

(g) Eat dried beans and legumes of all kinds, including peanuts, preferably unsalted.

(h) Walnuts and almonds are good for the brain.

(i) Restrict sugar and salt.

(j) Avoid hydrogenated vegetable oils

(k) Restrict processed food.

(l) Eat a relatively low-calorie diet.

(m) Soya products are low in fat and high in amino acids that make up neurotransmitters.

(n) Curd is probably the best dairy product, primarily because of its pro-biotic actions in the intestines.

(o) Meat is an acceptable food but by no means necessary.

(p) Fish is definitely a brain food at the top of the list. *A land with lots of herring* (a kind of fish) *can get along with few doctors* (Dutch proverb).

(q) Eat your protein first before you touch carbohydrates.

(r) Ayurvedic brain foods: Oats, oatmeal, oat flour, and oat milk are said to strengthen the brain and fortify the nervous system. Ghee made from cow's milk is credited with correcting mental disturbances caused by energy imbalances, improving memory and stabilising the intellect. Foods worth including as general items in your brainpower-building diet are apples, oranges, quince (a hard fruit that looks like an apple), rose water, ginger, cloves, chicken, fish, cow's milk, garlic and ginseng.

(s) "We all eat every day, so why not add a little Gingko Biloba or vitamin E or extra Choline to your diet. Your brain will thank you... Over the last 10 years I have found myself eating more protein – not red meat, mind you, but more protein from soybeans, fish and chicken. My body has told me through its various physiological channels, that it needs more protein. Lots more to keep the mind games rolling," according to Richard Leviton, author of *Brain Builders*.

Enthusiasm

Enthusiasm stimulates brain function. Vibrancy results from enthusiasm. Keep the fire of enthusiasm at white heat. You can achieve anything in this world through enthusiasm. Place within your mind and the deep recesses of your heart the need for enthusiasm. **Carry enthusiasm in your attitude and manner**, it spreads like a contagion. Every great achievement is the story of a flaming heart.

Environment

Interact with your environment. It may be with people or with nature. Grow a garden. Climb mountains. Listen raptly to the music of the birds. Talk to strangers without inhibition. The more you interact with the environment, the more proficient your brain becomes. It is possible to learn something from every kind of interaction. So go out and be active. Take a risk and do something new!

Exercises (Physical)

Physical exercise improves blood flow to the brain. This in turn helps accelerate brain activity. Brain functions can be improved only when blood vessels are unclogged and undamaged. Exercise helps keep blood vessels in prime condition. In addition, exercise strengthens the heart, lowers cholesterol level, and opens clogged arteries. It improves the mood and drives away stress and depression. Exercise can keep your brain young, vital and regenerative throughout your life. Walking, jogging, swimming, etc are best suited to improve brain function.

However, based on personal experience, I strongly recommend yogic exercises, preferably *Sirshasana* (standing on the head) and *Sarvangasana* (standing on the shoulders). These two *asanas* (Yogic postures) are suitable for youngsters. Adults can practise *Surya Namaskar*. I am a regular practitioner of Yogic asanas, pranayama and meditation. These unique exercises increase mental fitness, restore the brain's biochemical ability to lay down new memories and to focus intensely for extended periods. They also stimulate access to existing "remote" memories of long-past events. Yogic asanas, pranayama and meditation give the practitioner an immediate burst of energy – the after effects of this burst of energy can last up to 24 hours.

Flow Experience

This is a state of mind when you are totally absorbed in a task with deep concentration and commitment. A scientist may experience the flow state when he is totally absorbed in his research project. During a flow experience, you often cease to be aware of anything outside of what you are doing. Self-consciousness and self-doubt disappear. You are likely to lose all awareness of time. Flow experience is exciting and fulfilling, a reward in itself.

But flow experience has ramifications that go beyond mere pleasure; it expands your potential by its effects on the brain. People are more innovative about problem solving if they feel good. Feeling good helps us focus and persevere at tasks, because enjoyment has specific physiological effects on our brain. Any mental activity that "feels good" to you is a "reward" and will induce positive changes in the brain, ranging from the release of natural opiates to the consumption of more brain-enhancing oxygen and nutrients.

Forgetting

It is wise to consciously forget trivia, because they clutter your mind. One reason older people are forgetful about new information is that their minds are already crammed full.

Free Radicals

The modern environment is full of free radicals. New sources include X-rays, microwaves, nuclear radiation, toxic heavy metals (such as aluminium and cadmium, found in public water supplies), smog, chemical food additives, cigarette smoke, exhaust from automobiles, hydrogenated vegetable oils and artificial polyunsaturated fat substitutes such as margarine, non-dairy creamers, most bottled salad dressings and commercial cooking oils. The minute you consume any of these products (and they are widely used in prepared and processed foods and in restaurant and fast foods) they explode into free radicals in your system. When these oils are used in high-heat preparations (deep-fried foods and French fries), the heat causes them to oxidise much quicker, releasing more free radicals.

Where do most of these free radicals go? To your brain, which, among all other organs, is probably the most vulnerable to the onslaught of free radicals that enter your body.

Fruits

There are two varieties of fruits and their nutritional value for the brainpower diet varies widely. Dates and dried figs add a substantial amount of potassium, calcium and phosphorus to the diet, as well as magnesium, zinc and iron. These items are vital to build super brainpower.

Garlic

Garlic helps lower blood pressure. It purifies the bloodstream. Ingest three pearls of raw garlic in the morning along with four or five glasses of water for more brainpower. Research findings claim that garlic improves memory.

Ginseng

Ginseng has been used in China for more than 5,000 years as a health tonic. It is also called the elixir of life and touted as a miracle cure-all herb. It improves the way the mind works in several ways. It fights free radicals that damage brain cells. It improves blood circulation to the brain and thereby enhances its performance. Ginseng promotes better mental functioning by normalising heartbeat, blood sugar and blood pressure. It also increases the endocrine activity and metabolism rate, and resistance to drugs, alcohol, chemotherapy, and other toxins. It has anti-fatigue properties as well.

The other benefits of ginseng are: (a) improves athletic performance, (b) reduces the time needed to recover after exercising, (c) speeds recovery from stress, (d) helps overcome insomnia, (e) stimulates the immune system, (f) reduces cholesterol, (g) improves sexual performance, (h) helps the body ward off stress by acting on the adrenal glands, (i) increases norepinephrine levels during stress, (j) normalises blood sugar level, which leads to greater clarity of thought, (k) improves the level of blood circulation, which in turn contributes to improving the function of the hypothalamus and the pituitary glands.

Gingko Biloba

This herbal supplement (extracted from the leaves of the gingko tree) is considered the star of brain boosters. It is a free-radical scavenger with antioxidant properties. This keeps the cells in top working order. Acetylcholine is vital for memory function. Long-term use of gingko increases the number of acetycholine receptors in the brain. It has the ability to improve memory, thinking, reasoning and general mental alertness. Gingko increases blood circulation through the brain to boost the brain's energy and metabolism. No side effects from the leaf extract have been reported in scientific literature.

Many researchers say it is the most promising non-prescription "smart drug" or "cognitive enhancer". Gingko biloba has been approved in Germany for a decade to revive failing memory. The scientific buzz on gingko is so good that countless prestigious American scientists and doctors, many in their middle age, are now taking it, hoping to stave off memory loss as they grow older.

Dr Jerry Cott, age 52, chief of research on pharmacological treatment at the National Institute of Mental Health, USA takes 240 milligrams of gingko daily as "insurance" against declining memory. He thinks it is a reasonable and inexpensive precaution, based on current evidence. He also believes gingko has improved the mental function and well-being of his elderly mother who has Alzheimer's disease.

Holding the Breath

Dr Win Wegner, a scientist from Japan, did research on brainpower. He made youngsters practise inner retention (holding the breath after breathing in) underwater, preferably in a swimming pool. He made them practise inner retention for an hour everyday with frequent intervals of, say, one minute at a time. Thus they practised inner retention 60 times a day. After three months of this practice, he found that they had enhanced their IQ by 10 to 15 points. The span of awareness also increased.

This study proves that by holding the breath it is possible to stimulate your brain and also increase its power.

A Happy Frame of Mind

The brain functions more effectively with a happy frame of mind. Being happy is a choice, a decision. Although many seem to consider happiness a result of luck, accidental circumstances or the actions of other people, the fact is that people decide for themselves how happy they will be. Unhappy people decide, although unconsciously, to be unhappy. You can decide to be happy and begin to do the things that will enable you to be happy.

Health of the Body

You can be at your brainiest only when your body is in excellent condition. We have only one body. It is our primary duty to maintain it in good condition. Only through vibrant health can the flow of energy in our body be perennial. When energy level increases the brain functions more efficiently. People poison the body by taking pills and tablets for every conceivable minor disease. They tear it down by eating inappropriate rich foods and consuming harmful drinks. They torture the nervous system with pills to keep awake and pills to sleep.

Moreover, many flog their body to coax more out of their mind – skip sleep to finish a project, or rely on alcohol to stimulate brainpower for creative ideas. These strategies eventually sabotage the thinking process through the toll they exact on their body. You can't artificially improve your mental performance without taking time to let your body rest and rebuild. As the mind goes, so does the body. The two are in this game of life together, and your ability to keep them working as a team is a full-time challenge, one that involves everything you do. Your best thinking begins below the neck, because it is grounded in health – in a well-nourished, regularly exercised, relaxed body; one that supplies your brain with nutrients, oxygenated blood, and the stimuli that come from a variety of physical activities.

Techniques for Vibrant Health: The following techniques may be adopted to maintain excellent health:

(a) **Attitude:** The mind plays a tremendous role in maintaining good health. People with confidence and courage normally have good health. Fear, guilt and worries are ruinous to health. Have firm faith in the adaptive mechanism of your body. Don't be over-concerned with your health. Anxiety is debilitating. Most politicians live long and also maintain good health even in their ripe old age. The only contributing factor in their health is the confidence and courage they display in life.

(b) **Activate the Subconscious Mind:** Positive affirmations, such as "Day by day, in every way, I am getting better and better health", would activate your subconscious mind and thereby improve your health.

(c) **Generate Perennial Flow of Energy:** When the energy level is high your health will be excellent. You fall ill only when the energy level goes down. Positive thinking, purposeful living, a pinpointed goal in life and enthusiastic activity generate perennial flow of energy.

(d) **Moderation:** The general rule for excellent health is moderation in everything. Be conscious of this at all times in your wakeful state.

(e) **Diet:** This is a matter of habit depending upon our cultural background. One man's food may be another man's poison. The type of food we eat is not important, but it is important that we eat only foods conducive to good health. Vegetarian food is to be preferred over non-vegetarian food. The major intake should be fruits and vegetables. Eat only when hungry. Avoid overeating. When ill, fasting is best. Drink plenty of water, but not during meals.

(f) **Elimination:** Total evacuation of the bowels everyday is a must. Take two to three tumblers of hot water early in the morning. Along with it, consume three pearls of garlic. Not only is this good in cases of constipation, it also preserves the health of the heart. An alternative is a mixture of lemon, honey and ginger juice in hot water.

(g) **Develop Resistance Power:** Between four and six in the evening take three sweet limes, removing only the rind and seeds. This is far better than the juice, as it provides you fibre. The vitamin C in the sweet lime will develop resistance power in your body and prevent many diseases.

(h) **Sleep:** Sleep recoups your body and mind. Restful sleep is a must for all. But too much sleep would make you lazy and lethargic. *Sleep less and live longer* is the axiom. There is no general rule as to how many hours one should sleep. It all depends upon one's own lifestyle and work compulsions. Proper sleep contributes a lot in gaining excellent health.

(i) **Habits:** Develop habits conducive to good health and avoid those that are detrimental, such as smoking, drinking, drug addiction and sexual promiscuity.

(j) **Nature Cure:** For all minor illness take recourse to nature-cure methods. Avoid synthetic medicines as far as possible.

(k) **Yoga:** For at least half an hour daily, practise yogic asanas, pranayama and meditation. Yoga is an important ingredient for perfect health. Learn simple yogic exercises like *Surya Namaskar*. Never fail to practise pranayama and meditation. See the sections devoted to these two aspects. *Surya Namaskar* can be learnt from any book on Yoga, or by attending a course on Yoga.

(l) **Oil-pulling Technique:** Ancient Indian Yogis innovated this technique. Now it has been scientifically investigated and is considered a panacea for many ailments. It has preventive as well as curative effects. It is best done as soon as you wake up in the morning, before brushing your teeth. Take one teaspoon of purified sunflower oil or sesame oil (til oil) in your mouth. Gargle with this for about 20 minutes continuously till the oil becomes watery in the mouth with foam. Spit out the foam water and brush your teeth. Soap manufactured out of oil has a cleansing effect. Similarly, the oil-pulling technique will remove all germs from the mouth. The mouth is said to be the gateway to all diseases. In this way your mouth is purified and health is restored.

(m) **Stress Reduction Plan:** One of the simplest but effective ways to reduce stress is to dip your eyes in a bucketful of water. This can be done before bathing. Whenever you feel stressed, follow this technique for remarkable results.

(n) **Sex:** If there is genuine love and affection between a couple, sex can stimulate the body mechanism. According to research by gerontologists, people who have sex even in advancing years live longer. People with vibrant health can continue to have sex even at an advanced age.

Imagination

Imagination stimulates the brain. Sit in a chair. Keep an alarm clock on the table before you. Look at the clock for a few seconds. Then close your eyes. See the clock with closed eyes. Imagine it in space. Picture it much smaller than it is. Now change your mental picture by making the clock larger and larger. By doing this your brain is tremendously stimulated. The different sizes merely exercise different cells of the brain. By shifting the memory of your perceptions of these pictures you can stimulate a variety of brain cells. Imagining these visual images exercises your brain more than simply seeing them.

Intellectual Companions

It is necessary to keep the following intellectual companions, around the house: an unabridged dictionary, a thesaurus, an atlas and a set of encyclopaedias.

Interactive Dialogue

Reading should never be passive. As you read, make notes on the margin of the book of your own ideas related to what you read. When you write your own thoughts, reactions, comments, agreements and disagreements directly into the book, you already have an interactive dialogue with the author. Your brain continues to be active.

Internal Clock

An internal clock that is attuned to the daily pattern of darkness and daylight regulates many of the body's systems. These include heart rate, blood pressure, respiration rate and body temperature. Animals are generally oriented to either day or night, depending on their niche in the planet's ecology. We humans tend to be at our best by day. Not all daylight hours are equally friendly to mental work. As the body's various systems gear up and identify these personal peaks and valleys, you should be able to perform better. It is important to know when you are hot and when you are not.

IQ Tests

Be careful with the IQ scores. They do not accurately measure all aspects of brainpower. They are at best relative indicators of a few aspects of your potential brainpower but not the whole cerebral ballgame by any means.

Latent Learning

Although imagination stimulates the brain, some behaviour can be enhanced without actual physical rehearsal. Psychologists call it "latent learning", when you learn something without actually doing it. The process works since you have to stimulate the brain cells that control a particular physical activity to imagine yourself performing it. Suppose you are a basketball player. You can play everyday on the court but at night you can practise imagining you're playing every kind of shot.

Lead

Since 1945, when cars began using lead, the entire mental functioning of the United States and other countries has gone down quite a few IQ points. That's the enormous price paid for using leaded fuel. Man as a species is foolishly disseminating a poison throughout his environment, which inhibits the survival potential of his species. Lead may rank as the greatest environmental threat to human intelligence. It is impossible to avoid lead altogether. This toxic metal has been transmitted across the globe, throughout the oceans and even to the polar ice caps.

It accumulates in our bodies as well. Good nutrition can be important in minimising the effects of the toxin. And the corollary is also true: lead toxicity and its effects are aggravated by insufficient nutrients in the diet. Consuming enough iron and calcium is a good way to reduce lead damage. Zinc can also influence susceptibility to lead poisoning. Vitamin D discourages lead from building up in the body.

Luxuries

Many of the luxuries and so-called comforts of life are a positive hindrance to the effective functioning of the brain and are dispensable.

Massage

Many cultures have recognised that the "laying on" of hands is healing, relaxing and sensual. If you have someone who will massage your skin with a favourite lotion, that would be ideal. If not, you can massage yourself. Starting at your toes, and working your way up the body, including the arms and neck, up to your face, massage gently while relaxed. Music played softly may help and so may a darkened room. At least once a week (or more often if you are very tense or feeling "blue") have a massage. Again, the stimulation your brain receives from stroking the skin is soothing because your brain responds to it by releasing tranquillising endorphins.

Meditation

One of the best methods to boost brainpower is to practise meditation. Just sit and observe your thought processes. The mind is eternally restless, compulsively flitting from object to object, person to person, and place to place, most of them related to your personal life and problems. If you observe the functioning of your mind, you may notice that you are talking to yourself. Most of your self-talk revolves around your personal problems. It could be about your family or profession, your happiness and achievements, your problems and sufferings, etc. Your consciousness, which is a stream of thoughts and feelings, will be totally saturated with your personal problems.

As long as the mind is steeped in such thoughts and feelings there can be no real peace and tranquillity. You experience greater amount of stress in your life. Stress and tension will diminish the power of your brain. Unless stress is managed properly there is no way to improve the functioning of your brain.

One of the best ways to manage stress is to practise meditation, which is a process through which you shift your consciousness from your self to a state of thoughtlessness or "no mind". To put it simply, meditation helps the practitioner forget his self through a variety of techniques and keep his mind blank or free of thoughts. The moment the mind takes itself away from the self, it derives supreme joy and happiness.

Meditational techniques are especially good at balancing the "weather pattern" within the brain that enhances sharp thinking. This, perhaps, happens by enhancing the brain's ability to fire neurons in smooth, coordinated, organised patterns. Meditation improves mental power.

Here are some mechanisms by which this happens:

(a) Like the "smart drug" piracetam, meditation slows brain metabolism. This allows brain neurons to function more efficiently and use less energy. Better than piracetam, meditation promotes mental power without possible harmful side effects.

(b) Meditation can decrease blood levels of lactate. Excess lactate is known to cause anxiety and insomnia.

(c) Meditation increases levels of dehydroepiandrosterone (DHEA) – a marker of brain vitality.

(d) Meditation decreases blood pressure as well as cholesterol levels. This may lessen the risk of arteriosclerosis that might otherwise block the arteries and limit blood flow to the brain.

Meditation in Practise

A few meditation practices are given below:

(a) **Simple Meditation:** Just sit in a meditative posture for about 15 to 20 minutes, making your subconscious believe that you are 'meditating'. The main purpose is to acquaint you with self-discipline to sit quietly for a given length of time. This is a preliminary step for the practise of other types of meditation.

(b) **Sabdha Meditation:** *Sabdha* means sound. This meditation can be practised at any time, in any place and in any posture. Just focus your attention on the sounds you are able to hear. This can be practised even in a moving bus or train. Travel confines you to a particular seat. You can consider this an excellent opportunity to meditate. The drone of the moving bus or the chug-chugging of the train itself could be the object of meditation. Concentrate your entire attention on the sounds. When your thought slips off, bring it back and be aware of the sound only and nothing else.

(c) **Chitta Meditation:** *Chitta* means consciousness (stream of thoughts and feelings). This can also be practised in any place, at any time and in any posture. In this form you are supposed to observe your thoughts and feelings. Do not attempt to control or direct your thoughts. You act only as an objective observer of each thought, feeling and perception, etc that is being screened on your mental horizon. When a thought or feeling arises, simply observe it until it passes out of your visual space. Then you may wait for the next thought or feeling and observe it. Don't attempt to explore, follow-up or associate with any of the thoughts or feelings that are passing through your mind.

(d) **Trataka Meditation:** Keep an object before you, anything of your choice. Visualise it with closed eyes. Your thoughts should be continuously saturated with the object visualised. When it goes away from your visualisation bring it back and keep it in your consciousness. Apart from arresting the wavering mind, this type of meditation will also improve the power of your brain by developing concentration, imagination, will power and eyesight.

(e) **Zen Meditation:** This can be practised in any comfortable and restful posture. Focus on your breathing. When some other thought intrudes, push it aside. While being attentive to the breathing process, start counting your breath with every exhalation – one, two, three, etc. Your total attention is gently and firmly fixed on this one action of counting only.

But sequential counting becomes automatic and your thoughts would drift away from the focus on your breathing process. To counteract this, the counting may be varied slightly: count up to fifty and then count backward to one.

In Zen, the trainees are required to be aware of their breathing processes all the time. Since breathing is a continuous unbroken process you can concentrate non-stop on it until the end of the scheduled time.

If the breathing is deep and rhythmic a sort of vibration is created in the body, which will tone up your nervous system and thereby enhance brainpower.

Special Note on Meditation: Meditation should be treated as a way of life rather than a mere ceremony to be performed piously at an appointed time. Efforts should be made to occupy the mind fully with pure and positive thoughts. The mind should attend to only one thing at a time. Instead of brooding over personal problems, concentrate on some constructive activities that bring some beneficial results to humanity at large. The mind should be saturated with the theme "Love for all and hatred towards none". No event, however adverse, should disturb the mind. It should always be peaceful, tranquil and serene. This state without tension and stress is very conducive to maintaining excellent health. A stress-free mind stimulates brain functioning

Memory System

Don't clutter your mind with too many facts, figures and details. Create a few memory systems that will keep track of details. Write down some of the things you need at a later stage, like the telephone number of a friend. You may forget about it for the time being and take it up when needed. Keep your life well organised. Write down your schedule of activities for the day. Keep things that you may constantly need in their assigned places. Use reminder notes. Keep papers in a proper filing system. If your mind is uncluttered by daily details, you'll be amazed at how much clearer it will feel.

Mindfulness

A key to using your brainpower is to be alert, attentive and focused enough when it comes to having your neurons on the job. Start the day mindfully. Do it for a month. Mindfulness becomes a brainpower habit. The mindfulness exercise involves sensing, looking and listening. You are sensing your body, listening to the sounds you hear, actively looking at objects in your visual range and keeping some awareness on your breathing, all at the same time. This puts you into the present moment.

Practise this exercise anytime you need to regain your mental focus or before starting a big mental task, such as taking a test, writing a paper or doing calculations. Mastery of this exercise will train you to be more efficient and focused at learning.

Mind Mapping

This technique was developed in the early 1970s by Tony Buzon based on researchers' understanding of how the brain actually functions. This facilitates students to prepare notes from their textbooks. It is a whole-brain approach through which an entire subject can be displayed on one page. By using visual images and other graphic devices, mind mapping makes a deeper impression.

The brain often recalls information in the form of pictures, symbols, sounds, shapes and feelings. The mind map uses these visual and sensory reminders in a pattern of connected ideas, like a roadmap for studying, organising and planning. It can generate original ideas and easy recall. It is easier than traditional methods of note taking because it activates both sides of the brain. It is also relaxing, fun and creative. It is easier to remember the details from a mind map because it is written in a form that your brain naturally follows.

Making a Mind Map: Use coloured pens and start in the middle of the paper. If convenient, turn the paper sideways to provide more space. Then follow the steps given below:

(a) Print the main topic or idea in the middle and enclose it within a circle, square, or other shape.

(b) Add a branch extending out from the centre for each key point or main idea. The number of branches will vary with the number of ideas or segments. Use different colours for each branch.

(c) Write a key word or phrase on each branch, building out to add details. Key words are those that convey the art of an idea and trigger your memory. If you use abbreviations, be sure you are familiar with them so you'll instantly be able to identify what they stand for days or weeks later.

(d) Add symbols and illustrations for better recall.

(e) Write legibly or in CAPITAL letters.

(f) Make important ideas larger so they will jump out at you when you reread your notes.

(g) Underline words. Use bold letters wherever necessary.

(h) Construct your mind map horizontally to increase the amount of room you have for your work.

Preparation of mind mapping requires creativity and imagination. The brain is extraordinarily stimulated when it is engaged in creativity and imagination.

Minerals

(a) **Magnesium:** It averts the deadly consequences of calcium toxicity, maintains the metabolic viability of neurons and also minimises brain damage. It is a good free-radical scavenger. It helps increase the anti-oxidative power of vitamin E.

(b) **Selenium:** This is one of the most effective mineral antioxidants. It prevents oxidation of fat. Around 60 per cent of the brain is composed of fat. Selenium boosts immunity and improves circulation. The selenium levels in the blood typically decline as we age. After the age of 60 it drops by 10 per cent. The recommended dosage is 50 to 100 mg.

(c) **Manganese:** "If you have ever lost your car in a parking lot, or forgotten your keys in the door, you may need manganese, the mineral that helps overcome absent-mindedness. It's a memory-improver and nerve-nourisher, plus it helps produce thyroxin in the thyroid gland: 1 to 9 mg. a day are suggested," Sheila Ostrander, *Cosmic Memory*, page 256.

Music

Music is an important tool to improve and maintain brain and body functions. Research has established that music is very effective for concentration, memory skills and control of stress. Music is a readily available tool that produces unfailing results in improving your cognitive abilities.

Our body has rhythm and tempo, so does music. Therefore, music stimulates our nervous system very effectively. You get into the most fundamental of all musical rhythms with the continuous beat of your heart. The rhythm of music compels us to move and the tempo determines how fast it should be. It can accelerate the pace of your work and make it more fun. Just consider the popularity of jogging with earphones and of aerobic dancing with musical beats.

Listening is not just hearing. Hearing is passive, while listening is dynamic. Hearing refers to the sounds in your surroundings you are compelled to hear, whether you like it or not. But listening is a choice. The listener makes a conscious effort to understand the music and enjoys it. Here the intellect is involved. Listening goes beyond just appreciating the surface things. You identify the entire facets of the nuances of music. When you yourself sing you not only listen to your own music but add the physical functioning as well. You shake your head, move your fingers and tap your hands in sync with the rhythm of music. You perform mentally and physically. It demands concentration. There is a pervading aesthetic satisfaction. Your mind reaches a different level of consciousness where expansion of mind takes place with self-fulfilment and peak experience.

Music affects both your psychological and physiological states. When you are deeply involved in mental work your pulse and blood pressure may tend to rise. Your brain waves may go up and the muscles get tensed up. On the other hand, when you meditate and relax, your pulse and blood pressure decrease, and your muscles relax.

Normally, it is difficult to concentrate when you are relaxed and difficult to relax when you are concentrating.

To obviate this contradiction, Dr Georgi Lozanov, the creator of super-learning techniques, found that music was the key. Relaxation induced by specific music leaves the mind alert and able to concentrate. The music he found most conducive to this state is baroque music, like that of Bach, Handel, Pachelbel, and Vivaldi. These composers used very specific beats and patterns that automatically synchronise our minds with the bodies. For instance, most baroque music is timed at sixty beats per minute, which is the same as an average resting heart rate. Thus we see that music is undoubtedly a phenomenon to reckon with for boosting our brainpower.

Negative Ions

You feel sleepy on an airplane and energised at a waterfall. Negatively charged air molecules are found near waterfalls, mountains, on beaches, riverbeds, etc. The air in such places is pure and fresh. Scientists have found that the higher the negative ion level in an environment, the lower the serotonin level in your brain. Serotonin is what puts you to sleep. So, fresh unpolluted air, rich in negative ions, can lift the spirits and increase mental output.

Novelex (Novel Exercises)

Dr Arnold Scheibel, a neuroscientist, believes firmly that novel tasks stimulate brainpower. Challenge the brain with anything new and different. He advises people to do things they have never done before. He himself recently took up sculpture. Novelty is very biologically stimulating to the brain. The Novelex programme calls for providing the brain with novel, unique and different experiences on a day-to-day basis. They should constitute non-routine and unexpected experiences using various combinations of your physical senses – vision, hearing, taste, smell, and touch. It differs from other types of brain exercises, such as solving puzzles, riddles, magic squares, mathematical/accounting problems and memory exercises. Novelex makes use of the five senses in novel ways to develop the brain's natural drive to form associations between different types of information.

In the book *Keep Your Brain Alive*, authors Lawrence C Katz and Manning Rubin make use of the word *Neurobics* to describe the exercises referred to here as Novelex. I prefer to use the word Novelex as all the exercises given below are based on the principle of novelty.

Adults normally go through life in remarkably fixed routines. Most of their actions are perfectly predictable and free from surprises. The result is that our brain's ability to make new associations declines. Routine behaviours are almost subconscious in nature and performed using a minimum of brain energy. Thus the brain gets little exercise. The power of the cortex to create new associations is, therefore, not properly utilised. **The human brain hungers for novelty.** It is designed to respond to new information coming from the outside world. The brain gets stimulated when novel and unexpected stimuli are presented. It is what turns the brain on. In response to novelty, cortical activity is increased in more and varied brain areas. This strengthens synaptic connections, links different areas together in new patterns, and pumps up the production of neurotrophins.

Novelex is neither passive nor routine. It uses the senses in novel ways to break out of everyday routines. The latest brain imaging studies have clearly established that novel tasks activate large areas of the cortex, indicating increased levels of brain activity in several distinct areas. Of the five senses with which we establish contact with the outside world, we mostly rely upon only the two senses of vision and hearing. The other senses of taste, smell and touch are rarely used. Novelex makes use of all the senses.

Any exercise programme demands time. One should be highly motivated to set aside a specific time slot to take up a physical exercise programme. Fortunately, Novelex programmes are designed in such a way that they fit into what you do routinely, without taking extra time. They are recommended as a lifestyle choice, not as a crash course or a quick fix. Simply by making small changes in your daily habits you can turn daily routines into 'mind-building' exercise. However, Novelex exercises should not become a routine affair.

The following techniques constitute Novelex:

(a) *Involve one or more of your senses in a novel way.* We normally use the sense of vision for most of our routine activities. When the sense of vision is blocked, you are forced to use other senses. For example, get dressed for office with your eyes closed.

(b) *Have bath with the eyes closed.* All activities relating to bathing should be done with the eyes closed. Your hands will probably notice varied textures of your own body, which you were not aware of earlier.

(c) *Make liberal use of your non-dominant hand.* If you are right-handed, start using your left hand for most routine work like brushing your teeth, buttoning clothes, opening the door, turning on switches, etc. A variety of things can be done using your left hand. When you use your left hand, your right brain is stimulated, which we rarely stimulate.

(d) If you are habituated to using a ball pen, *use pencil or an ink pen.*

(e) *Take a different route to your office/school or college.* When you go on your normal route your brain gets on automatic pilot. When anything is done automatically without any awareness, the brain is not stimulated at all. When you take a new route all your senses must be alert while you drive.

(f) If you want to read fast, silent reading is recommended. But if you want *to stimulate your brain reading aloud helps.* You may also ask a friend to read to you. When you read aloud or listen to someone read, you use very different circuits than when you read silently. Brain imaging clearly showed three distinct brain regions lighting up when the same word was read, spoken or heard. For example, listening to words activated two distinct areas in the left and right hemispheres of the cortex, while speaking words activated the motor cortex on both sides of the brain as well as the cerebellum. Just looking at words activates only one area of the cortex in the left hemisphere.

(g) If you are a South Indian, *occasionally try North Indian dishes.*

(h) You may also *change the order of eating*, say, start with dessert. Your brain will thank you for such a change.

(i) Try to *identify the items of food on your plate only through the sense of smell.*

(j) *When you go for a walk in the morning, try to change the route everyday.* If you walk in a park, try to walk with your eyes closed.

(k) If you plan a vacation, *visit new places and interact with new people.* The more you travel the more would be the brainpower. Travel broadens the vision and perception and also stimulates the brain. Travelling is something novel for the senses.

(l) *Write something creative.* Creative activity stimulates the brain.

(m) *Learn sign language.* This would not only help you communicate with challenged people comfortably, but stimulate your brain because of the novel way of communicating.

(n) In office or at home, once in a way, *reposition the furniture and furnishings.*

(o) *Learn a new language, acquire new skills* and also try to understand and operate any new gadgets.

(p) *Constantly change the pattern of whatever you are doing.*

Obstacles

Stress, depression, alcohol use, dietary style, inadequate nutrition, chronic constipation, brain allergies, high blood pressure and hypertension are obstacles to brainpower. Correct these negative factors.

Oxygen

The brain that is short of blood is apt to be short on oxygen as well. In older people, the lungs as well as the heart tend to become less efficient. Exercise has the ability to deliver more oxygen to people in their middle and late years. The brain needs oxygen to oxidise glucose in the production of electrical energy – the very sparks that are our thoughts and feelings. It is also believed that certain neurotransmitters are highly dependent on oxygen for their production. While the brain makes up only two per cent of the body's weight, its demands for oxygen are enormous – 20 per cent of the body's share, ranging up to 50 per cent when we are fast-growing children. Shallow breathing and clogged arteries may leave the brain gasping for air, in effect. Symptoms range from confusion, a lack of mental vitality and senility.

Poisoning the Brain

Learning what can poison your brain is as important as learning what will improve brain function. Even aspirin, which is universally accepted as being safe, can be poisonous to brain cells if a large dose is taken. The following are classes of potentially toxic or poisonous prescription drugs: psychiatric drugs – barbiturates, bromides, Benzodiazepama, phenothiazines, Haloperidol, lithium; drugs used in general medicines: digitalis preparations, analgesics, antidiabetic agents, cimetidine, methuyldopa, Inderal, Reserpine, Symmetrel, drugs with anti-cholinergic actions, etc.

Power Thinking

To build your intellectual power, abandon conventional ways of thinking. Re-examine all your most cherished beliefs. Above all, let go of your previously held conclusions, because most of our conclusions are not ours at all. They come from others – our families, the media, and the state. Open your mind to the infinite possibilities of new ideas. Learn how to sharpen your innate power of comprehension, insight, intuition and sensory perception. Develop confidence in your mental abilities. Separate the wheat of truth from the chaff of mere opinions. Build your brain to use power thinking instead.

Pranayama

The effective functioning of the brain largely depends upon one's energy level. One of the best ways to increase your energy level is to practise Pranayama.

Prana is the vital force pervading the entire universe, representing the principle of cosmic energy. It exists in all beings, from the highest to the lowest, both animate and inanimate. Prana is the cause of the growth process in this world. Prana manifests itself as electricity, gravitation, magnetism, etc. The actions of the human body, nerve currents and thinking force are operated through prana.

In normal breathing our intake of prana is very little. Ancient rishis and yogis innovated a variety of techniques to draw more prana from the atmosphere and also to preserve the excess prana in the solar plexus. These techniques are called Pranayama.

Pranayama may be defined as a systematic approach designed to bring about perfect control over the flow of prana throughout the body by the application of certain methods and techniques achieved through the regulation of physical breathing.

Practise of Pranayama: There are more than a hundred varieties of Pranayama techniques. For boosting brainpower, I present three techniques here:

(a) **Ujjayi Pranayama:** Sit comfortably. Inhale through both nostrils by gently contracting the neck, the chin slightly touching the chest bone. The air will not have any free flow. It will be obstructed at the pharyngeal area. There will be a sibilant sound when the air is passed through the back wall of the mouth.

This pranayama can be practised in any place, at any time and in any posture. It removes tiredness and fatigue. It is also highly beneficial for persons suffering from high blood pressure. They can do it in a reclining position. When blood pressure is controlled, the brain functions effectively.

(b) **Nadi Shodhana Pranayama:** Sit comfortably with the left arm on the left thigh. The thumb and ring finger should gently touch each side of the nose to close the left and right nostrils and the index and middle fingers should touch the forehead.

Follow this procedure: Inhale through the left nostril for a count of 3, retain for 6 counts, then exhale through the right nostril for a count of 6, outer retention for 3 counts; inhale through the right nostril for a count of 3, inner retention for 6 counts, exhale through the left nostril for 6 counts, outer retention for 3 counts. This completes one cycle of *nadi shodhana pranayama*.

Have three to five rounds.

Benefits: Brings calm and tranquillity and purifies the nerves. The bloodstream is purified of toxins and the blood receives a larger quantum of oxygen than in normal breathing.

Due to alternate breathing the flow of prana in the Ida (left) and Pingala (right) nadis is equalised. Right nostril breath stimulates the left hemisphere of the brain and the left nostril breath activates the right hemisphere. This pranayama technique makes optimum use of both the brain hemispheres.

(c) **Kapalabhatti Pranayama:** Sit comfortably. Close both fists with the thumb inside and place them on the thighs touching each other. This is *maha mudra*.

Inhale in a mild, slow and long manner and exhale quickly and forcibly by contracting the abdominal muscles with a backward push as many times as possible. Inhalation and exhalation occur simultaneously. Inhalation is mild and silent and exhalation is forceful and vehement.

Beginners can do it 20 to 30 times and the number should be increased gradually.

It cleans the respiratory system and nasal passages. Asthma is relieved. Carbon dioxide is eliminated. It aids heart function.

Every single cell in the brain is stimulated to an extraordinary level. This is one of the best techniques to improve your intelligence and creativity.

Prayer

Believe in God. Prayer can heal. Meditative prayers that focus on feeling the presence of God stimulate the brain. This in turn results in miraculous cure of certain incurable diseases. Prayer works directly on the brain cells.

Reading

Many neurological researchers believe that reading is uniquely beneficial for the brain. Reading requires active engagement of the mind and imagination. It powerfully stimulates both hemispheres of the brain, as well as the limbic system. Only 20 per cent people read books.

Questions

Intelligence is what makes us ask "Why?" Therefore, ask as many questions as possible to boost your brainpower. That gives us the capacity to reason.

Reflexology

The human body mechanism is very intricate. It is said that the right brain takes care of the functioning of the left side of the body and the left brain deals with the right side. There is a subtle connection between the left and the right side of the body. We have seen that if we breathe through the left nostril, the right brain is stimulated and the right nostril breath stimulates the left hemisphere of the brain. Similarly, we have access to more brainpower at the tips of our thumbs and big toes. This technique comes from the natural therapy called reflexology. There is a complete energy map of our body on the bottom of each foot and the palm of each hand. The technique involves manipulating and massaging points on your feet and hands to stimulate your brain.

Press the big toes and little toes: Sit comfortably in a chair with bare feet. Keep your right leg on the left thigh. Catch hold of its big toe with your right thumb and index finger and massage it for about three minutes. Similarly, massage all the other toes on your right leg. Now reverse the position and follow the same sequence with your left foot. Try this brainpower toe massage for seven minutes each day. Massaging the left side stimulates the right hemisphere of the brain and vice versa.

Press your thumbs and fingers: The brain's reflex points are located in your thumbs and fingertips. Hold your right thumb with your left thumb and index finger and massage it for about three minutes. Similarly, massage all the other fingers on your right hand. Spend one minute on each finger. Likewise, massage your left hand with your right hand.

Repetition

Through repetition, nerve cells become connected and myelinated to make recall of information easy. Without occasional review, myelin (a whitish fatty substance forming a sheath around many nerve fibres) begins to dissolve.

Rhythms

The brain has its own rhythms of activity and rest every day. You have natural highs and lows of brain functions every 90 to 120 minutes. Your body gets into these rhythms called ultradian rhythms. The brainpower diminishes at least for 20 minutes. Mental skills rise and fall according to the rhythms. Give 20 minutes' break for improved functioning of your brain.

Selenium

It is an elemental metal that has antioxidant properties because its outer electron shell will accommodate electrons common in the destroying of free radicals. In studies, it has been shown to act synergistically with vitamin E as an antioxidant.

Sex

Studies have shown that sexual stimulation releases endorphins in the brain and not only eases tension, but also relieves the pain of arthritis and other ailments. Studies on animals have shown that the stimulation of the genitals increases brain metabolism. So, if you need a good excuse to have sex, there it is! Sex will help you think better.

Silence

The mind keeps flitting from place to place, person to person and ideas to ideas. There is an inner monologue continuously going on in our mind. It is the constant narration and commentary we hear every minute inside the head as if somebody is constantly talking, complaining and chattering. The chatter wastes a great deal of valuable energy. Silence is the only solution. If you don't communicate with others, either orally or in writing, it is outer silence. But only inner silence will bring you tranquillity. How do you ensure such silence?

Sit comfortably in a chair. Close your eyes. Observe your thoughts and feelings. Be aware of what is going on in your mind. The mere observation itself would make you reduce the chatter of the mind. Silence saves energy and increases brainpower simply because you no longer waste it.

Sleep

Sleep is more than a mental vacation when we drift off into unconsciousness each night. During sleep the brain goes through a series of physical and psychological processes that restore both body and mind. Sleep is generally considered as a natural phenomenon that allows the brain and other organs of the body to recover from wear and tear of daily life. Recent research proves that the brain does not rest during sleep. On the contrary, electrical activity, oxygen consumption, and energy expenditure in certain regions of the brain actually increase. One purpose of the extra brain activity during sleep is to reinforce memories.

Sleep not only serves to retain memories through protein replacement, which counteracts the continual wear and tear, sleep provides the brain with a way to shuffle excess information into a convenient plan of neural storage. If we don't have sufficient sleep over a period of time, our memories would shrink. Without sleep, we lose much of our ability to transfer the day's information into long-term memories. A catnap after lunch is enough to charge up for the rest of the afternoon.

This does not mean that if we sleep more we get more brainpower. In reality, too much sleep would bring lethargy and sap your energy. To sleep well, we must have a relaxed frame of mind. There is no general rule as to how many hours one should sleep. It all depends upon one's lifestyle and work schedules. People who hold high positions and those desirous of accomplishing great things in life sleep less than those who drift aimlessly in life.

Because I am absorbed in writing books and conducting training programmes, I get up normally at 3.30 in the morning and continue to work till 10 to 10.30 at night without feeling tired. On those days when I don't have a training programme, I may take a catnap after lunch. I attribute my level of energy to the practice of Yoga, pranayama and meditation. In all my training programmes I insist on all participants practising the yogic exercises of asanas, pranayama and meditation. **From personal experience, I am fully convinced that yogic practices boost brainpower considerably.**

Sleeping Pills

Any clinical agent that produces drowsiness is called a sleeping pill. They work by depressing the central nervous system. Sleeping pills may help you sleep through the night, but there is a clear difference between drug induced and non-drug sleep. Sleeping pills are useful in treating mild and transitory insomnia, as might occur after a stressful event or a trip to another time zone. Long-term treatment with sedative sleeping pills alone almost never works. Close medical supervision and adoption of lifestyle and behavioural changes, including treatment of underlying medical or psychological causes, is necessary.

Smart Drugs

Steven Fowkes, editor of *Smart Drug News*, defines smart drugs as "any drug or nutrition that enhances aspects of mental performance". When we speak of 'cognitive enhancement', we wish to include all the myriad mental functions that go into making us what we are. This would not only include such obvious aspects like intelligence and memory, but also include items such as sex, relations, sleep, immune function, and neuroendocrine regulation. These are all vital aspects of human health and well-being that are related to the functioning of the brain. Gingko biloba, ginseng, vitamins, etc are considered smart drugs.

Smoking

Smoking may cause changes in the structure of the lungs that lower oxygen concentration in the blood. This can lead to reduced function of brain cells.

Spirituality

People who are spiritual – that is, connected to some inner core of faith and hope – show positive effects on brainpower similar to those of people who meditate. Spirituality is definitely useful in boosting brain efficiency.

Stress

Stress destroys the ability to concentrate in several ways:

(a) Stress causes release of both **norpinephrine** and **serotonin**. Both these neurotransmitters are necessary for sharp thinking, but prolonged, excessive release depletes their store and eventually leaves the brain in short supply.

(b) Stress releases **hydrocortisone**. Scientists have found that excess hydrocortisone damages the hippocampus, which is the centre of learning and remembering. Chronic hydrocortisone release will actually shrink brain size through cell death.

(c) Stress stimulates the **glutamate receptors** and causes excitotoxicity of the brain cells, which are pushed into overtime activity. This condition fatigues brain function, and in chronic conditions will eventually also cause cell death.

(d) Stress interrupts **sleep patterns**. Loss of sleep immediately affects one's ability to concentrate.

Manage stress by developing a wholesome philosophy in life: For effective functioning of the brain it is essential to manage stress by adopting the following philosophy in life:

(a) **Live in the Present:** "Now" is all there is, and the future is just another present moment to live when it arrives. The present moment is inseparable from us. At any point of time you cannot do away with the **NOW**. This is the only thing that **is always with you**. The past is dead and the future is unborn. People who experience stress are those who live either in the past or the future. Guilt of the past and worries of the future always haunt them. Those who know how to grab the present moment and maximise it have chosen a stress-free, effective and fulfilling life. It is a choice each of us can make.

(b) **Accept the Inevitable:** Many things in life are beyond our control. Our birth itself could be considered as fate. Death of our beloved ones may occur any moment in our life. Accidents can happen to anybody at any moment. These are things for which we are not responsible. Many things cannot be changed. All things that are inevitable in life should be accepted gracefully; otherwise we shall be tormented with stress, tension and worries.

Reinhold Niebur's poem, which Alcoholics Anonymous calls the Serenity Prayer, is worth committing to memory and repeating often:

God, grant me the serenity
To accept the things I cannot change,
The courage to change the things I can
And the wisdom to know the difference.

(c) **You are what you are:** Our relationship with others should be one of neither superiority nor inferiority. The repetition of the following statements would reinforce in you this philosophy:

No one is superior to me
No one is inferior to me
I am what I am.

(d) **You are unique in this world:** Be convinced that you are something new in this world. Be proud of being unique. "Make the most of what Nature gave you. In the last analysis all art is biographical. You can sing only what you are. You must be what your experience, your environment and your heredity have made you. For better or for worse, you must cultivate your own little garden, and play your own little instrument in the orchestra of life," said the legendary motivator Dale Carnegie.

(e) **There is no success or failure in life:** Success or failure is a matter of **attitude** in life. We should take life as it unfolds. Our main business in life is to involve ourselves deeply in the creative activities in which we are keenly interested without bothering much about reward or result. There is no question of failure. Failure might suggest that we have to make some more attempts to accomplish the task in hand. Develop the attitude: **"When I win I win, when I lose I learn."** Every second of our wakeful state provides a wonderful opportunity to learn one thing or another. Every failure should be considered as deferred success. Never quit. Pursue your project till you succeed in your attempts. Winston Churchill said, "NEVER, NEVER, NEVER, NEVER, NEVER GIVE UP."

(f) **Whatever happens is for your good:** Think in a positive way that whatever happens to you in life is for your own good. An ancient story is related here to illustrate this point:

A king and his minister went into a jungle to hunt. A tiger attacked them and in the fight the king lost a finger. He was in agony, but the minister said, "Everything is for our good." At this the king got angry and pushed him into a shallow dry well. Falling into the well, the minister uttered, "Everything is for our good."

After a while, some tribals captured the king. They intended to sacrifice him, but on second thought freed him when they realised he was minus a finger. Then the king came to the minister, rescued him from the well and asked, "Why did you say 'Everything is for our good' when I pushed you into the well?"

The minister said: "Your Majesty was saved because of the loss of a finger, for the sacrificial victim should not have any blemish. But if I had not been pushed into the well, they would have sacrificed me."

(g) **Convert minus into plus:** One of the best ways to manage stress is to convert minus into plus. **Count your blessings** and not your troubles. Develop an attitude to convert minus into plus.

(h) **Don't expect justice and fairness:** There is virtually no justice in this world. The general trend is that might is right. The prisons are filled only with those who are not able to defend their case with money. People in power do far worse things but escape due to the power they hold. Few politicians in India have been punished for fraudulent and corrupt practices. Only poor and helpless people are regularly punished and victimised. Therefore, don't expect justice and fairness at every turn of life.

(i) **Expecting gratitude is unrealistic:** People may tend to forget the good you have done them. It is unwise to expect that everyone should be grateful.

(j) **Accept mysticism gracefully:** We cannot reason out everything that happens in our life. A certain amount of mystery pervades the life of everyone. In an accident many died and a few escaped. Why? We don't know. Accept it.

(k) **The best is yet to be:** This is one of the best principles to be adopted in the sphere of personal growth and development. We should always be satisfied with what we have but not with what we are. It is better to strive hard to improve our potential, capabilities, efficiency, character, etc. Every minute of our wakeful state should be utilised for shaping our personality for a happy and prosperous life through a stress-free attitude. *Kaizen* is the word given by the Japanese for continuous steady growth and development in life.

Stimulants

Stimulants like coffee, tea, tobacco in any form, alcohol and other recreational drugs like marijuana and cocaine have a stimulating effect for a short spell of time. They even help focus the mind. But in the long run the power of the brain will be sapped. Frequent use of these items may cause even cell death.

Sugar

Your brain is a glutton for the sweet stuff in your blood. Your nerve cells depend on a normal range of blood sugar – not too much, not too little – to function optimally. Indeed, nothing is more critical to your brain than the type of sugar – glucose – that circulates in your blood and cells, and is largely determined by what you eat. Nerve cells can't survive and thrive without blood glucose, also known simply as "blood sugar". It is nature's original smart drug and mood elevator. It can perk up your memory, concentration, and learning abilities. It can help take away the blues and lower your irritability. Deficiencies of blood glucose can cause the brain to slow down and malfunction.

Yet high levels of blood sugar can be extremely detrimental. It can impair brain performance and memory. It can disturb the functioning of your brain and mangle brain cell architecture, accelerating mental decline as you age.

Sunlight

Studies reveal that our bodies need to be exposed to **full-spectrum light** – not just the few parts of the spectrum radiated by most lamps – if we are to feel energetic and to perform at our best. Light somehow reaches into the brain and stimulates our thoughts and emotions. Fluorescent tubes are in wide use in offices, factories, and schools because they are luminous – providing roughly four times more illumination than an incandescent bulb of the same wattage. Tubes transmit less heat, too. But you don't need bright lights to accomplish what the sun does naturally. Daylight is a free and bountiful resource. Therefore, **go outdoors early and late in the day** and open the curtains to let the sunshine flood in to make your brain function more effectively.

Tax Your Brain

Ella Tuttle Mattheson, a 102-year-old columnist for the *Clinton*, a local newspaper in Clinton, Michigan, once said, "My memory is as sharp today as it ever was. It's just that I have to **tax it a little more**. But then, I've got a lot more to remember than anyone else."

Dorothy Fuldheim, a feisty American broadcaster in her ninth decade (90), commented, "It gets my goat when people say it's remarkable how bright I am at my age. The more I use my brain, the sharper it gets."

Thinking

Walking might be regarded as physical exercise, and everyday thinking can be termed as brain exercise. The human mind has a capacity to learn in direct proportion to the challenges its owner is willing to meet, because the brain has physical and chemical properties that allow it to change for the better. The more we choose to use our brains the better our brain will function throughout our lives. The more we think, regardless of our age, the bigger our brains become and better their function. The brain has the ability to keep growing throughout life.

Travel

Visiting new places and interacting with strangers is a good way to coax the brain into making new dendritic connections. What you should mostly avoid is simply doing nothing. Those who remain active preserve cognitive function and brain metabolism. Travel provides abundant opportunity for mental exercise, which is vitally important for brain regeneration.

TV Programmes

The common pastime for many people is to watch TV. Watching too much television makes the brain passive and erodes cognitive skills. An exception could be quiz programmes. Excessive TV watching is particularly harmful to the development of the right brain, spatial intelligence in children. Children who watch television for long hours tend to avoid traditional childhood hobbies, such as art projects, building, or sports and games. These activities require three-dimensional, spatial reasoning skills. Spatial intelligence has been declining among schoolchildren for several decades.

Another terrible effect of television, and also of our hectic lifestyles, is that too few people today take time to read.

Twirling

It is a kind of brain-building exercise not unlike bodybuilding in its results. Twirling or spinning may even stimulate your neurons to "grow" more dendritic connections, which increases the already complex neuronal network and thus the physical basis for higher IQ. Now start slowly spinning around from left to right moving your entire body. Spin around six times and then stop. You will probably be dizzy. Over the next several weeks, try to work your way up to being able to spin 21 times comfortably, without feeling dizzy. Consider practising this twirling exercise an hour before the crucial brainpower test.

Vitamins

Vitamins are essential for boosting brainpower. Vitamin B (B12, B1, B3, and B6) is the most important one for optimal brain function. B vitamins are water-soluble. This means that for the most part they are not stored in the body for long. Therefore, the supply of vitamin B should be replenished frequently. B12 is particularly effective in boosting brainpower.

It is smart to take vitamin C, and it may make you even smarter. Researchers have only recently discovered that vitamin C is a very strong antioxidant that passes readily through the blood-brain barrier. It is concentrated in high levels in brain tissue and contributes to the creation of neurotransmitters, such as dopamine, and protects cells from free-radical damage. Numerous studies show that higher amounts of vitamin C in the bloodstream boost cognitive performance apparently at all ages and protect against age-related brain degeneration, including Alzheimer's disease and stroke.

Vitamin E is the mother of all antioxidants. In partnership with the mineral selenium, it neutralises free radicals that accelerate the stress process. For antioxidant benefits a dose as much as 800 to 1600 IU (international unit) of vitamin E per day is recommended.

Yantra

This is called Sri Yantra. This is one of the most powerful techniques innovated by Indian yogis for stimulating the brain and improving concentration.

Sri Yantra

Practise of Sri Yantra: Sit in a relaxed position. Do *bhakya kumbaka* (outer retention) as follows: Breathe in, breathe out. Don't breathe in immediately. Pause. This provides good relaxation. Now look at the centre white dot of the Sri Yantra. You will see that your attention goes to different geometric figures. As you continue to look at the Yantra, your attention keeps moving from one geometric figure to another. This activity increases communication between the left and right hemispheres of the brain. This technique will increase the power of concentration.

✡✡✡

Part Three

BRAINEX
EXERCISE FOR THE BRAIN

Mental Exercises

The brain continues to develop throughout our lives, not by the addition of neurons, but by the accumulation of experiences that change the chemistry and structure of our synapses. Brain exercise is a direct form of experience that is extremely conducive to effective functioning of the brain. Mental exercise increases the number of dentrite connections among brain cells. Solving puzzles, riddles, mathematical and accounting problems can be considered good mental exercises.

In this book only puzzles and riddles are given, as they do not require any specialised knowledge like mathematics and accounting. Make an attempt to answer all of them. Only after solving the puzzles on your own should you look for the answers given at the end of Part Three (page 95 onwards).

1. Often talked about, never seen, ever coming, never been, daily looked for, never here, still approaching, coming near. Thousands for its visit wait, but alas for their fate, though they expect me to appear, they will never find me here. What am I?
2. If 20 men, 20 women and 20 children eat 20 kg of rice in 20 days, in how many days would one man, one woman and one child eat 1 kg of rice?
3. A woman is 5 years younger than her husband who is 9/2 the age of his son. The woman is four times the age of her son. What are the ages of the woman, her husband and their son?
4. Mary's mother had four children. The first child was named June, the second July and the third August. What is the name of the fourth child?

5. What word can be placed in front of the outer five to form five new words or phrases? Each dot represents a letter.

UP

TRIP

(. . . . .) ABOUT

SHOULDERED

NUMBER

6. Three friends went to a hotel for accommodation in one room. The clerk told them the rent for a three bedroom would cost Rs.300. They paid Rs.300, each of them contributing Rs.100. Later the clerk realised he had committed a mistake. The room rent was Rs.250 only. The clerk gave Rs.50 to the steward to be returned to the three men. The steward gave the amount to them. They took Rs.10 each and the balance Rs.20 they gave the steward as tip. The men have now paid Rs.90 each. This makes Rs.270. The steward received Rs.20 and the total comes to Rs.290. What happened to Rs.10?

7. Divide 50 by half and add 20. From the sum minus 35. What do you get?

8. A frog fell into a well 32 feet deep. Each day it jumped 2 feet up the sidewall and slid back down 1 foot each night. How many days did it take for the frog to jump out of the well?

9. The ages of a father and son add up to 55. The father's age is the son's age reversed. How old are they?

10. Four friends left one slice of cake in the kitchen and went into the next room to play cards. During the next one hour, each friend left the room for a few minutes and then returned. At the end of two hours, all four went back into the kitchen and found that the slice of cake was missing. Each of them made the following statements:

A said: "B ate it."

B said: "D ate it."

C said: "Who me? Can't be!"

D said: "B is lying when he says I ate it."

Only one statement is true – which one?

11. A mother sent her son to the river to fetch exactly 3 litres of water. She gave him a 9-litre can and a 4-litre can. Show how the boy can measure exactly 3 litres of water using nothing but those two containers.

12. A bottle and a cork together cost Rs.150 and the bottle costs Rs.100 more than the cork. How much does each cost?

13. What number should replace the question mark?

7	5	9	18
6	3	7	21
4	3	9	?
7	4	8	24

14. Rearrange the letters of GROW NO LINSEED to spell one single word.

15. What is the next number after the following?

    4 9 25 49 (?)

16. A word can be placed in the brackets that have the same meaning as the words outside. What is it?

    AVERAGE (. . . .) STINGY

17. Four cars came to a crossroads at the same time, each coming from a different direction. All the drivers were in a hurry and proceeded fast without stopping at the crossroads. They did not crash into each other. How is this possible?

18. A child learning the English alphabet can draw only straight lines. How many capital letters can he write?

19. The following is a one-inch line:

A ————————— B

Can you make this smaller without touching or rubbing it?

20. What do you throw out when you want to use it, but take in when you don't want to use?

21. In each of the following sentences is hidden the name of a country. Can you name these countries?

(a) His painstaking efforts were much admired.

(b) Couples wed entirely of their own accord nowadays.

(c) There's no catch in any of these sentences.

(d) The greenhorn sheriff ran celebrities' town.

(e) Fighting against the strong wind, I advanced very slowly.

(f) They easily scan a day's order forms in half an hour.

(g) The money that I bet you will go to charity if I win.

(h) The company Dabur made excellent tonic for brainpower.

22. In the following questions, digits do not carry their true value but are allotted artificial values:

If 35 + 48 = 40

23 + 34 = 24

15 + 25 = 26

11 + 21 = ?

23. A's watch is running 10 minutes slow but he is under the impression that it is only 5 minutes slow. B's watch is running 10 minutes fast, but he's under the impression that it is only 5 minutes fast. Both A and B reach a particular place at 4 according to their

calculations. At what time would they reach there if their watches showed the correct time?

24. What relationship does your father's only brother's wife's only brother-in-law share with you?

25. 3295 : 4931 : 6567

    Which series below has the same relationship as the series above?

    3752 : 4852 : 6943

    3721 : 4923 : 6490

    4296 : 6326 : 7892

    2345 : 3981 : 5617

    2346 : 3852 : 6423

26. What belongs to you, but others use it more than you do?

27. A man walks 2 km east, then 2 km south, followed by 2 km east, 3 km north and 4 km west. How long must he walk and in what direction to reach his starting point?

28. Which single number can be placed at the question mark?

15	6	5
13	3	9
8	2	?
20	7	13

29. Given below are six-letter words. Form the longest word possible using only the letters of the six-letter word in each case. Each of the letters in the original word may be used as often as needed, or not at all. For instance, in the first case, using the letters TORIES, you might make the word RESISTOR. See if you can create a new word from the letters of the original words.

(a) TORIES
(b) PUNTER
(c) TINGLE
(d) COINED
(e) DEPART

30. I cultivate banana in my kitchen garden. One day I took a bunch of bananas to the market. I sold half for tomatoes and ate 4 bananas myself. Then I sold half of the remaining bananas for apples and ate 3 bananas. Afterwards I ate one banana and sold half of it for carrots. This left me with 5 bananas. How many bananas did I take to the market to sell?

31. Name the choice that provides the answer in the following:

If 6 = 18
7 = 28
8 = 40
Then 12 = ?

32. What is it that when you take away the whole you still have some left?

33. X and Y are two brothers. B is A's brother but A is the mother of X. What is B to Y?

34. In a family of many children one child drinks everything – Coffee, Tea and Horlicks – and another child does not drink any of these. Of the total children two drink Coffee, four drink Tea and three drink Horlicks. Of these one drinks only Tea, another child drinks Tea and Horlicks, another drinks only Horlicks and one drinks Coffee and Tea. How many children are there in the house?

35. If 50 men travel 100 km in 24 hours, in what time would 100 men travel that distance, the speed in each case remaining the same?

36. If you cross out all unnecessary letters in the following string of letters, a logical sentence will remain: AALLLOUGNINCEACELSSSEANRYTELNETCTEERS.

37. What is the next letter?

```
                    O
                  O T
                O T T
              O T T F
            O T T F F
          O T T F F S
        O T T T F S S
      O T T F F S S Next alphabet?
```

38. A man was taking a walk outdoors when it began to rain. He did not have an umbrella and was not wearing a hat. His clothes were soaked, yet not a single hair on his head got wet. How is this possible?

39. A bus leaves from the Bangalore bus stand every 30 minutes. An enquiry clerk told a passenger that the bus had already left ten minutes earlier and the next bus would leave at 9.35 AM. At what time did the enquiry clerk give this information to the passenger?

40. A and B were excitedly describing the result of one particular track event at the Olympic Games in Sydney. There were three contestants: C, D and E. A reported that C secured the first position whereas D came in second. B on the other hand asserted that E came in first while C secured the second position. However, neither A nor B had given the correct result. Yet, each of them had given one correct statement and one incorrect statement. What was the actual placement of the three contestants?

41. Given below is an inverted triangle made up of ten coins. Change its position by keeping the base down and face up. Only three coins should be changed.

10 9 8 7

4 5 6

3 2

1

42. How can 4 be half of 5?

43. How can you make the following equation true by drawing only one straight line?

$$5 + 5 + 5 = 550$$

44. Mr X earned Rs.63,000. One-third of it went to taxes. The rest he invested in shares, which appreciated by one-half. Two-thirds of this amount went for business expenses. Of the remaining amount the government took an additional two-thirds for the current year's tax. Is he left with any money?

45. A very affluent newly married couple went to church one Sunday. On their return they found that someone had robbed their safe. They questioned all the staff working in their mansion. The cook said that he was busy preparing the lunch. His assistant said that he was helping the cook. The third servant claimed she was preparing the table for lunch. The gardener said that after finishing his work in the garden, as usual he was sorting the day's postal mail. The couple had a strong suspicion that one of the workers in the house was not being truthful and could be the culprit. Whom did they suspect? Why?

46. A word I know contains six letters. Remove just one letter and twelve is what remains. What is the word?

47.

Star	Star	Moon	10
Moon	Flower	Sun	
Moon	Sun	Star	9
8	12		

2 Stars + 1 Moon = 10

1 Moon + 1 Sun + 1 Star = 9

1 Star + 2 Moons = 8

1 Star + 1 Flower + 1 Sun = 12

Find out the value of One Star, One Moon, One Sun and One Flower.

48. What three letters change a girl into a woman?

49. Five boys are sitting in a row. A is on the right of B. E is on the left of B but he is on the right of C. A is on the left of D. Who sits first from the left?

50. A student was asked to multiply a number by 3 and then add 8 to it. Instead, he first added 8 to it and then multiplied it by 3. The answer that he got was 69. What should have been the correct answer?

51. A traveller was on his way to Bangalore when he came to a fork in the road. He was wondering which way to go. Suddenly, two men appeared. He came to know that of the two, one man would always tell the truth and the other would always tell lies. Unfortunately, the traveller did not know who would tell the truth and who would tell lies. What question could he ask one person that would indicate the right road to Bangalore?

52. Due to a shipwreck A, B, and C were washed ashore on a small island. Reaching the shore exhausted, they all fell asleep. A woke up first and saw that a box of apples had been washed ashore. He ate one-third the apples and went back to sleep. Next, B woke up and seeing the box of apples, ate one-third of what was left

and fell asleep. C woke up next and assumed that the other two hadn't eaten any apples, so he ate one-third of what remained. When C had finished, there were eight apples left over. How many apples were in the box originally?

53. A little boy lived with his parents on the 10th floor of a block of flats. When he went to school in the morning he used to take the lift from the 10th floor to the ground floor. But when he returned from school at the end of the day he went in the lift only as far as the 7th floor, and then walked up the stairs to the 10th floor where his flat was. Why?

54. If 9th April falls two days after tomorrow, that is Wednesday, what would be the last day of the month?

55. A, B and C went gambling. A had as much money as B and C together. C brought only 1/6 of the total pool. At the end of the game, A was left with as much money as B, whereas C got twice that of A and B. If C had brought Rs.100 in the beginning, what was the amount brought by all the gamblers and how much did they take home?

56. If it takes 6 hours for four men to dig 8 holes, how long does it take one man to dig half a hole?

57. Five friends – A, B, C, D, and E – entered a contest to guess how many jellybeans were there in a jar. A's guess was 30, B said 28, C 29, D 25, and E 26. Two were off the mark by 1, another was off by 4, and one by 3. But one was correct. How many jellybeans were there in the jar at the store?

58. The maker does not want it; the buyer does not use it; and the user does not see it. What is it?

59. There are 25 people in an empty, square room. Each person has full view of the entire room and everyone in it without turning his head or body, or moving in any way (other than the eyes). Where can you place an apple so that all but one person can see it?

60. In a room there are cats and hens. They have 15 heads and 50 feet. How many cats are there?

61. Decode the following: WOHS RETUO NAHT WOLG RENNI HTIW EFIL RUOY YFITUAEB.

62. A birthday party was held for Mr X. He had to cut the cake. Seven of his close friends gathered to celebrate his birthday. They imposed one condition on him. He should cut the cake into eight pieces but he was allowed to make only three straight cuts. How could he do this?

63. A man was looking at a portrait on a wall and said: "Brothers and sisters I have none, but this man's father is my father's son." At whose portrait was he looking?

64. How many times will you write the numeral 2 if you write all the numbers from 201 to 300?

65. If you start with the number one and use only whole numbers, how far do you have to count before you need to use the letter "a" in spelling a number?

66. Do this mentally, not on paper. Take 1,000 and add 40 to it. Now add another 1,000. Next add 30. And another 1,000. Then add 20. Now add another 1,000. Next add 10. What is the total?

67. In a certain code LEAP YEAR is written as NGCR AGCT. How is CENTURY written in this code?

68. Sixteen squares are given here. Fill them with the following: four blue (B), three red (R), three green (G), three yellow (Y), and three white (W). Arrange the counters in such a way that no two of the same colour are in line vertically, horizontally and diagonally.

69. The owner of a winery died of old age. In his Will, he left 21 beautiful rosewood barrels – seven filled with wine, seven half full, and seven empty – to his three sons. The wine and barrels were to be split so that each son had the same number of empty barrels. There are no measuring devices handy. How can the barrels and wine be evenly divided?

70. From the word MONDAY, can you make another six-letter word?

71. Study this paragraph and all things in it. What is vitally wrong with it? Actually nothing in it is wrong. But you must admit that it is most unusual. Don't just zip through it quickly. But study it scrupulously. With luck you should spot what is so particular about it and all words found in it. Can you say what it is? Tax your brain and try again. Don't miss a word or a symbol. It is not all that difficult.

72. Two notorious liars, A and B, live in a village. But they lie only on certain days of the week. A lies throughout Monday, Tuesday and Wednesday. B always lies on Thursday, Friday and Saturday. One day a man visited the village, met the liars, and asked A what day it was. He answered: "Well, yesterday was one of my lying days." Then the visitor turned to B and asked him the same question, to which B answered: "Yesterday was one of my lying days also." What day is it?

73. Whoever makes it, does not reveal it. Whoever takes it, does not know it. Whoever knows it, does not want it. What is it?

74. A man was found shot dead in his study. He was slumped over his desk with a gun in his hand. There was a cassette recorder on his desk. When the police entered the room and pressed the play button on the tape recorder, they heard: "I can't go on. I have nothing to live for." Then there was the sound of a gunshot. Is it a murder or suicide?

75. Here is a 9-letter word STARTLING. Can you find 8 more words by just removing one letter at a time?

76. Prepare 8 x 8 = 64 squares. Place in them 8 coins in such a way that no two coins are in the same horizontal, vertical or diagonal.

77. A farmer was on his deathbed. He had 17 horses. He wanted to bequeath the horses to three of his sons. He wished to give one-half of the horses to his eldest son. The next son was to receive one-third. And the last son was to get one-ninth of the horses. After issuing these instructions the farmer passed away. No one knew how to divide the horses. They did not wish to sell or kill any of the horses. Just then their neighbour came riding along on his horse and listened to their problem. Immediately the neighbour thought of a clever solution to the problem of dividing the horses as per the dead man's instructions. How did he do it?

78. Two babies were born on the same day with the same mother and father but are not twins. How is it possible?

79. Connect the following 25 points with only eight straight lines so that all 25 points are touched once and only once.

0 0 0 0 0

0 0 0 0 0

0 0 0 0 0

0 0 0 0 0

0 0 0 0 0

80. Decode the following numbers: 8-21-13-9-12-9-20-25 19-16-5-1-11-19 9-14 19-9-12-5-14-3-5.

81. The Sultan of Oman wants to send a huge diamond to his brother in the mail but he is afraid that someone will steal it during transit. He has a box that can be fitted with two locks, and he has lots of padlocks and keys. But his brother does not have the keys to the

Sultan's locks. How can he send the diamond securely locked, and still allow his brother to open the box?

82. What everyday word in the English language is most often pronounced incorrectly?

83. Relief workers went to a village affected by floods with a truck containing 100 loaves of bread. The small village had a population of exactly 100 people. The elders of the village decided that the bread should be distributed as follows: Each child would receive half a loaf of bread, each woman two loaves and each man three. The relief workers distributed the loaves as per the instructions of the elders. How many men, women and children lived in the village?

84. In eight pieces of paper or card, write the digits 1 to 8, one digit per piece of paper, and arrange as shown in the first diagram, so as to leave one empty space. Digits are to be moved one at a time, and may only be moved into the empty space from an adjoining space with no jumping allowed. Following these rules can you arrange the eight pieces into the order shown in the second diagram? What is the least number of moves that you can do it in?

7	5	6
8	2	1
4	3	

First Diagram

1	2	3
4	5	6
7	8	

Second Diagram

85. A murderer is condemned to death. He has to choose between three rooms. He is told the first is full of raging fires, the second is full of mad assassins with loaded

guns, and the third is full of huge lions that have not eaten for three months. Which room should he choose?

86. From Chennai to Bangalore the distance is 375 km by rail. Katpadi is on the line between them and is 150 km from Chennai. At 12 noon a train sets out from Chennai and reaches Katpadi at 13.15 PM. It halts there for 15 minutes and then goes to Bangalore, arriving at 15.00 PM. Another train leaves Bangalore at 12.30 PM and runs non-stop to Chennai at an average speed of 100 km per hour. How far from Katpadi do the two trains pass each other and at what time?

87. CROSS + ROADS = DANGER

The above statement is a simple addition in disguise. Each letter stands for one and only one digit and no digit is represented by more than one letter. By ingenuity, reason, perseverance or sheer good luck, can you work out which digit each letter stands for?

88. There are numerous words where the first letter can be deleted to leave another complete word. For example, detaching the first letter from CACHE leaves ACHE. List as many letters as you can.

89. Jason was excited when he saw his name on his friend's calendar. His friend pointed out that Jason's name was on every calendar. Can you figure out where?

90. An old widow, Mrs Y arranged a party to celebrate her 100th birthday. She invited her children and their spouses, her grandchildren and their spouses and all her great-grandchildren. In all, 86 people attended the party. Can you give a break-up of the persons who attended the party – children, grandchildren and great-grand children?

91. How would you rearrange the letters in the words "new door" to make one word?

92. Six glasses are in a row. The first three are filled with milk, and the last three are empty. By moving only one glass, can you rearrange them so that the full and empty glasses alternate?

93. A man walks into his bathroom and shoots himself right between the eyes using a real gun with real bullets. He walks out alive, with no blood anywhere. He did not miss and he wasn't Superman. How did he manage this feat?

94. Write the correct answer in the following:

LUNCH = 6

DINNER = 8

SUPPER = 8

BREAKFAST = ?

95. A is younger than C but older than B. D is younger than B. C is older than A, but younger than E. Who is the youngest and who is the oldest?

96. Here below you find $3 \times 3 = 9$ squares in which the numbers 1 to 9 are filled. Arrange these numbers so as to create a magic square with a total of 15 on all sides – horizontally, vertically and diagonally.

1	2	3
4	5	6
7	8	9

97. A magic square is one in which a set of different numbers in a square formation are in such a way that the rows, columns and main diagonals add up to the same figure. But can a square of figures be formed so that when the figures are multiplied together the rows, columns and main diagonals give the same number? Fill the numbers that give you 27,000.

98. Prepare a similar 3×3 square in which you should get 216, when the figures are multiplied. The maximum

number that can be used should be 36. The same number should not be repeated.

99. The following is a 16-square table in which the numbers from 1 to 16 are inserted. Arrange these numbers in such a way that the totals of all the sides, horizontally, vertically and diagonally, will be 34.

1	5	9	13
2	6	10	14
3	7	11	15
4	8	12	16

100. The following is a 25-square table in which numbers from 1 to 25 are inserted. Arrange these numbers in such a way that the totals of all the sides, horizontally, vertically and diagonally, are 65.

1	2	3	4	5
6	7	8	9	10
11	12	13	14	15
16	17	18	19	20
21	22	23	24	25

Answers

1. Tomorrow.
2. 20 days.
3. Husband 45 years, wife 40 years and child 10 years.
4. Mary.
5. ROUND.
6. You have been misled into remembering Rs.300 as the cost of the room. The actual cost is Rs.250. Each paid Rs.90, which works out to Rs.270, i.e., Rs.250 + Rs.20 they paid the steward.
7. 85. When you divide 50 by half you will get 100 and not 25, as you may have thought!
8. 30 days – on the 30th day it jumped two feet and came out of the well.
9. The father is 41 and the son is 14.
10. C ate the cake. It is impossible for A, B or C's statement to be the only one that is true. If A's statement that B ate it is true, then C's statement is also true. If B's statement that D ate it is true, then C's statement is also true; then no one statement can be true. Therefore, C's statement is false.
11. To get 3 litres of water, first fill the 4-litre can twice and pour into the 9-litre can. Now the 9-litre can contains 8 litres of water. Then fill the 4-litre can for the third time and pour one litre into the 9-litre can. Now the 4-litre can will have exactly 3 litres of water. The 9 litres of water in the 9-litre can should be thrown out.
12. The bottle costs Rs.125 and the cork costs Rs.25.
13. Reading from left to right, first column – second column × third column = fourth column. 4 – 3 = 1 × 9 = 9. 9 is the answer.

14. ONE SINGLE WORD can be formed by rearranging GROW NO LINSEED – both contain 13 letters.

15. The numbers in the row are squares of 2, 3, 5, and 7, all prime numbers. The next prime number in that series would have to be the sixth prime number 11. The answer, therefore, is 11 squared, or 121.

16. MEAN.

17. All the four cars turned to the left side.

18. A E F H I K L M N T V W X Y Z – other letters are curved B C D G J O P Q R S U.

19. Draw a bigger line than the one-inch line.

20. An anchor.

21. The answers:

    (a) Hi**s pain**staking efforts were much admired. (Spain)

    (b) Couple**s wed en**tirely of their own accord nowadays. (Sweden)

    (c) There's no cat**ch in a**ny of these sentences. (China)

    (d) The greenhorn sherif**f ran ce**lebrities' town. (France)

    (e) Fighting against the strong w**ind, I a**dvanced very slowly. (India)

    (f) They easily s**can a da**y's order forms in half an hour. (Canada)

    (g) The money tha**t I bet** you will go to charity if I win. (Tibet)

    (h) The company Da**bur ma**de excellent tonic for brainpower. (Burma)

22. 10. (3 + 5 + 4 + 8 = 20 × 2 = 40). Similarly 1 + 1 + 2 + 1 = 5 × 2 = 10.

23. A's watch 4.05 and B's watch 3.55.

24. He is your father.

25. 2345 : 3981 : 5617 : At each stage add 1636.

26. Your name.

27. He has to walk one km towards the south.

28. In each column, the sum of the upper two columns is equal to the sum of the lower two columns. 15 + 13 = 28 / 8 + 20 = 28. Similarly, 5 + 9 = 14 – 13 = 1 / 1 is the answer.

29. The answers:

    (a) RESISTOR (TORIES)

    (b) ENTREPRENEUR (PUNTER)

    (c) INTELLIGENT (TINGLE)

    (d) COINCIDENCE (COINED)

    (e) PERPETRATED (DEPART)

30. 64 bananas (64/2 = 32-4 = 28/2 = 14-3 = 11-1 = 10/2 = 5).

31. 108. The pattern is 6 × 3 = 18; 7 × 4 = 28; 8 × 5 = 40; 9 × 6 = 54, 10 × 7 = 70; 11 × 8 = 88; and 12 × 9 = 108.

32. The word WHOLESOME.

33. Uncle.

34. The answer:

Child	Coffee	Tea	Horlicks
A	Yes	Yes	Yes
B	No	No	No
C	No	Yes	No
D	No	Yes	Yes
E	No	No	Yes
F	Yes	Yes	No

A drinks all, B does not drink anything, C drinks only Tea, D drinks Tea and Horlicks but not Coffee, E drinks only Horlicks and F drinks Coffee and Tea and not Horlicks. The total number of children is 6.

35. 24 hours.

36. Remove unnecessary letters and you will get A LOGICAL SENTENCE.

37. E – One, Two, Three, Four, Five, Six, Seven and *Eight*.

38. The man was bald!

39. At 9.15 AM.

40. E first, D second and C third.

41. Only 1, 10 and 7 should be changed as shown below:

        1
      9   8
    4   5   6
  10 3   2   7

42. The Roman numeral IV appears in the middle of the English word FIVE – F(IV)E.

43. 5 + 5 + 5 = 550

    5 4 5 + 5 = 550

44.

Amount earned	Rs. 63,000
One-third for taxes	Rs. 21,000
	Rs. 42,000
One-half appreciated	Rs. 21,000
Total amount available	Rs. 63,000
Two-thirds of this for expenses	Rs. 42,000
Balance	Rs. 21,000
Two-thirds of this went for taxes	Rs.14,000
He has a balance of	Rs.7,000

45. The gardener was lying. No post is delivered on Sundays.

46. Dozens. Remove 's' and you will have a dozen.

47. Star 4, Moon 2, Sun 3, Flower 5.

48. Age.

49. C – Sitting position = CEBAD.

50. 53 – That is, 69 – 24 = 45 + 8 = 53.

51. The traveller would pick either man, point to the other and ask the first man, "Which road would he say is the right road to Bangalore?" If the man who is asked is the one who speaks the truth, he would indicate the wrong road because the truthful man knows the liar would lie about it. If the man he is asking is the liar, he would definitely indicate the wrong road. Either way, no matter whom he asked, he would be able to get the wrong road. Once the wrong road is known, he can easily choose the right road!

52. 27 apples. Explanation: 27 – 9 = 18 – 6 = 12 – 4 = 8.

53. He is too short to reach beyond the 7th floor button!

54. It is clear that 9th April is Wednesday. The next Wednesday is 16th, the Wednesday after that is 23rd and the last day, 30th April, falls on Wednesday.

55. Answer:

Gamblers	Brought	Took back
A	Rs. 300	Rs.100
B	Rs. 200	Rs.100
C	Rs. 100	Rs.400

56. No one can dig half a hole.

57. There were 29 jellybeans in the jar.

58. Coffin.

59. Place the apple on one person's head.

60. There are 10 cats.

61. Beautify your life with inner glow than outer show.

62. The first two cuts should be made like an X. This would divide the cake into four pieces. He should make the third cut horizontally through the middle of the cake, not on thse top. The third cut should divide the cake into eight pieces. Now there are four pieces on the top tier and four more underneath it.

63. The portrait of his son.

64. The answer: 99 times + 02, 12, 20, 21, 22, 23, 24, 25, 26, 27, 28, 29, 32, 42, 52, 62, 72, 82, 92 (total 19) = 118 times.

65. Till you count the number one thousand, you don't use the letter "a"! It may surprise you, but it is true. You can check this out yourself.

66. Do you get 5,000? OK, so do most other people. But the correct answer is 4,100. Check it with your calculator.

67. EGPVWTA. In the alphabetical order one letter should be skipped (e.g. L = N; E = G; A = C) to unlock the code.

68. The answer:

Y	B	W	G
G	R	Y	B
B	W	G	R
R	Y	B	W

69. Four half-full barrels are poured into another two of the empty barrels. This results in nine full barrels, three half-full barrels and nine empty barrels. Each son gets three full barrels, one half-full barrel, and three empty barrels.

70. DYNAMO.

71. The paragraph has been constructed without using one of the important vowels E.

72. Thursday. On Thursday A is supposed to tell the truth. Therefore, he said yesterday (Wednesday) was a lying day. But for B it is a lying day. So he said yesterday (Wednesday) was a lying day. In reality this is not. But on Thursday he is supposed to tell lies.

73. Counterfeit money.

74. It was a murder. The cassette had begun playing from the beginning of the man's statement. Who would have rewound it, except the murderer?

75. Starling (T is removed), which is a species of bird, Staring, String, Sting, Sing, Sin, In and I.

76. The solution:

O							
							O
			O				
						O	
		O					
					O		
	O						
				O			

77. The neighbour added his horse and made the total 18. The first son received 9 horses, which is one-half, the second son received 6 or one-third and the last son got 2 horses, which is one-ninth. The total horses distributed worked out to 17. The neighbour then mounted his horse and rode away.

78. They are not twins but triplets, since there was a third child.

79. Answer:

0	0	0	0	0
0	0	0	0	0
0	0	0	0	0
0	0	0	0	0
0	0	0	0	0

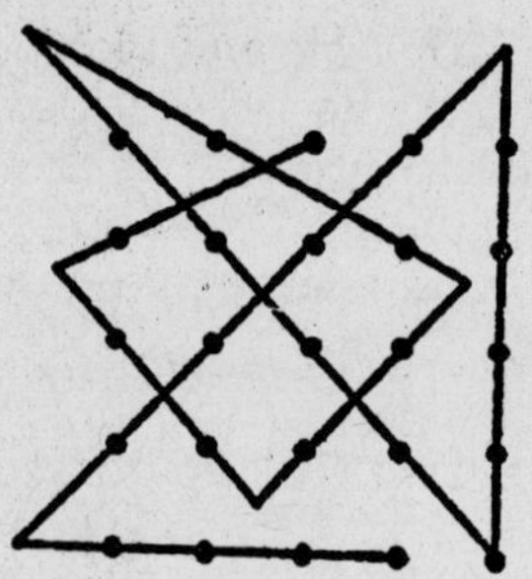

80. The answer: *Humility speaks in silence.* The numbers are given in alphabetical order. Example: 8 = H, 21 = U, 13 = M, etc.

81. The Sultan puts the diamond into the box, secures it with one of his locks and sends the box to his brother. His brother then attaches one of his own locks and returns it. When the Sultan receives the box back, he removes his lock and sends it back to his brother.

82. Incorrectly!

83. 74 children, 15 women and 11 men.

84. It can be done in 26 moves. Since there is only one empty space, it is necessary to list the digit moved each time: 1 2 3 1 2 6 5 3 1 2 6 5 3 1 2 4 8 7 1 2 4 8 7 4 5 6.

85. The third. Lions that have not eaten for three months would obviously be dead!

86. The two trains pass each other at 2.00 PM, 75 km from Katpadi.

87. The answer: 96233 + 62513 = 158746.

88. Some words are:

(a) ALONE – LONE

(b) FOX – OX

(c) FLUTE – LUTE

(d) FOWL – OWL

(e) ARISE – RISE

89. He was looking at the first letters of these months: **J**uly, **A**ugust, **S**eptember, **O**ctober, **N**ovember.

90. Children 5 + spouses 5; grandchildren 15 + spouses 15; great-grandchildren 45 + Mrs Y = 86.

91. One word!

92. Pick up the second glass and pour the milk into the fifth glass and then put it back in the second position.

93. He shot his reflection in the bathroom mirror.

94. 12 – count one for consonants and two for vowels.

95. D is the youngest and E is the oldest – DBACE.

96. The answer:

8	1	6
3	5	7
4	9	2

97. The answer:

6	225	20
100	30	9
45	4	150

Example: 6 × 225 = 1,350 × 20 = 27,000; 6 × 100 = 600 × 45 = 27,000. Likewise, the calculations for the rest of the figures give the same result, 27,000.

98. The answer:

2	36	3
9	6	4
12	1	18

= 216

99. The answer:

1	15	14	4
12	6	7	9
8	10	11	5
13	3	2	16

= 34

100. The answer:

23	6	19	2	15
10	18	1	14	22
17	5	13	21	9
4	12	25	8	16
11	24	7	20	3

= 65

Part Four deals with the preparation of Magic Squares.

✡✡✡

Part Four

MAGIC SQUARES TO BOOST BRAINPOWER

Magic Squares

I am much fascinated with the concept and preparation of magic squares. I find it stimulating and interesting. One of the best ways to boost your brainpower is to work out a variety of magic squares. To stimulate my brain I prepare magic squares for fun and pleasure. The impact it has in activating my brain cells is phenomenal. One can develop concentration and will power by preparing magic squares.

Definition

A magic square may be defined as an intriguing device where a big square is divided into a number of smaller squares where a set of different integers (whole numbers) is arranged in a particular pattern to form a grid in such a way that the sum of the numbers in every row, in every column and the diagonals adds up to the same number. The numbers that fill the magic squares are generally consecutive numbers. The big square is known as the magic square and the smaller ones containing the numbers are termed as cells or boxes.

The History

There is a story about the genesis of magic squares. In China, many centuries before the birth of Christ, a tortoise crawled out of the Yellow River. On its back people discovered a strange pattern of dots. When these dots were converted into numbers the sum of the numbers vertically, horizontally and diagonally was found to be the same. People were surprised at its magical constituents. They tried to construct similar patterns with different sets of numbers and also with varied patterns of squares.

The first person to take up the construction of magic squares was Cornelius Agrippa (1535–1486 BC) from China. These magic squares were associated with the heavenly bodies – the Sun, Moon, Mars, Mercury, Jupiter, Venus and Saturn. In the seventh century AD the construction of magic squares was taken up in France on a scientific basis with the application of mathematical principles. They became very popular in the Arab countries in the tenth century AD. Magic squares were mostly popularised in India by the famous mathematician Bhaskaracharya in the twelfth century AD. He contributed a lot in the construction of a variety of patterns of magic squares. In the sixteenth century AD this became popular in the Western world.

The Magic Spell

People in the past as well as the present believe in the magic spell of magic squares. A magic square of a particular pattern is engraved on precious metals like silver and gold and kept with them to bring good luck and fortune. It works effectively on those people who believe in it.

Construction of Magic Squares

Odd Number Squares

Odd number squares constitute 3 x 3 = 9, 5 × 5 = 25, 7 × 7 = 49, 9 × 9 = 81, etc. They follow a similar pattern. The minimum number that can be accommodated in these squares can be computed as follows:

3 × 3 = 9 – 1 = 8/2 = 4 + 1 = 5 × 3 = **15**

5 × 5 = 25 – 1 = 24/2 = 12 + 1 = 13 × 5 = **65**

7 × 7 = 49 – 1 = 48/2 = 24 + 1 = 25 × 7 = **175**

9 × 9 = 81 – 1 = 80/2 = 40 + 1 = 41 × 9 = **369**

11 × 11 = 121 – 1 = 120/2 = 60 + 1 = 61 × 11 = **671**

The following are the magic squares worked out with the minimum number.

Nine-cell Magic Square (3 × 3)

The total is 15.

8	**1**	6
3	5	7
4	9	2

How to construct it:

1. Start with number 1, just above the centre cell of the box.
2. Number 2 should be placed on the corner box at the bottom right.
3. Numbers 3 and 4 should be arranged as shown in the above magic square.
4. If you multiply the middle number 5 with 3 you will get the total for all sides (5 × 3 = 15).

Twenty-five Cell Magic Square (5 × 5)

The total is 65.

23	6	19	2	15
10	18	**1**	14	22
17	5	13	21	9
4	12	25	8	16
11	24	7	20	3

How to construct it:

1. Start with 1 just above the middle box.
2. Number 2 should be placed one box above diagonally.
3. When number 2 reaches the top, number 3 should be placed down at the right corner box.

4. Then number 4 should be kept at the left side above the corner box.
5. The next number 5 should be placed diagonally.
6. Number 6 should be placed vertically by skipping one box above.
7. Then number 7 should be brought down.
8. Numbers 8 and 9 should be placed diagonally.
9. After reaching the right end, number 10 should be placed on the left side.
10. First priority should be given in filling the diagonal empty boxes.
11. After reaching the dead end, number 11 should be placed at the bottom right corner.
12. The subsequent numbers 12, 13, 14 and 15 should be placed diagonally.
13. After reaching the top, number 16 should be brought down on the same vertical line above the corner box.
14. Based on the pattern explained above prepare 7 × 7 and 9 × 9 squares starting with number 1.
15. Check your answers with the squares given below.

Forty-nine Cell Magic Square (7 × 7)

The total is 175.

46	15	40	9	34	3	28
21	39	8	33	2	27	45
38	14	32	**1**	26	44	20
13	31	7	25	43	19	37
30	6	24	49	18	36	12
5	23	48	17	42	11	29
22	47	16	41	10	35	4

Eighty-one Cell Magic Square (9 × 9)

The total is 369.

77	28	69	20	61	12	53	4	45
36	68	19	60	11	52	3	44	76
67	27	59	10	51	2	43	75	35
26	58	18	50	**1**	42	74	34	66
57	17	49	9	41	73	33	65	25
16	48	8	40	81	32	64	24	56
47	7	39	80	31	72	23	55	15
6	38	79	30	71	22	63	14	46
37	78	29	70	21	62	13	54	5

The main features and construction of odd number squares:

1. Observe how these magic squares are constructed.
2. They follow a similar pattern.
3. To get the minimum total number we have to start with 1 and go on placing numbers 2, 3, 4, 5, etc till all the boxes are covered as per the explanations given above.
4. The first number should be commenced at one cell above the centre cell.
5. The total that can be accommodated depends upon the pattern of squares. For example in a 3 × 3 = 9 squares, the total should be divisible by 3. Similarly, the total should be divisible by 5 in a square composed of 5 × 5 = 25. This principle holds good for all the odd number squares.

How to construct with different totals

Once the starting number is known, it is easy to construct by following the guidelines given above. To find out the starting number the following procedure may be followed:

1. Find out the code number for every pattern. The code number can be worked out as follows:

   $3 \times 3 = 9 - 1 = 8/2 = 4$. **4** is the code for $3 \times 3 = 9$ squares

   $5 \times 5 = 25 - 1 = 24/2 = 12$. **12** is the code for $5 \times 5 = 25$ squares

   $7 \times 7 = 49 - 1 = 48/2 = 24$. **24** is the code for $7 \times 7 = 49$ squares

   $9 \times 9 = 81 - 1 = 80/2 = 40$. **40** is the code for $9 \times 9 = 81$ squares

2. The code numbers are useful to find out the starting number. For example, to get a total of 18 in a 9-cell magic square pattern the following method should be followed:

   Divide 18 by 3. The quotient is 6. The code for a 9-cell square pattern is 4. Deduct 4 from 6 and we get 2. The number 2 should be the starting number to get a total of 18 in a 9-cell magic square. This can be worked out as follows:

   The total is 18.

9	**2**	7
4	6	8
5	10	3

   If the total is 66, what should be the starting number? This can be worked out as follows: $66/3 = 22 - 4 = 18$. 18 is the starting number.

   The total is 66.

25	**18**	23
20	22	24
21	26	19

The same procedure should be followed for constructing a 25-cell square, 49-cell square, 81-cell square, etc. One example of each is given:

25-cell Magic Square (5 × 5)

To get a total of 130, the starting number should be calculated as follows:

130/5 = 26 – 12 = 14. The code for a 25-cell magic square is 12 and the starting number should be 14. The magic square is constructed as follows:

The total is 130.

36	19	32	15	28
23	31	**14**	27	35
30	18	26	34	22
17	25	38	21	29
24	37	20	33.	16

49-cell Magic Square (7 × 7)

To get a total of 777 in a 49-cell magic square (7 × 7) the starting number should be calculated as follows:

777/7 = 111 – 24 = 87. Number 87 is the starting number.

132	101	126	95	120	89	114
107	125	94	119	88	113	131
124	100	118	**87**	112	130	106
99	117	93	111	129	105	123
116	92	110	135	104	122	98
91	109	134	103	128	97	115
108	133	102	127	96	121	90

Pick a number of your choice and work out an 81-cell square (9 × 9) and 121-cell square (11 × 11).

Even Number Squares

Even number squares are of two types. One is composed of completely even numbers like 4 × 4 = 16-cell squares, 8 × 8 = 64-cell squares, 16 × 16 = 256-cell squares, etc. They follow one particular pattern. The other type is composed of 6 × 6 = 36 squares and 10 × 10 = 100 squares. This type follows a different pattern.

16-cell squares (4 × 4), 64-cell squares (8 × 8) and 256-cell squares (16 × 16)

The minimum number that can be accommodated is worked out as follows:

4 × 4 = 16/2 = 8 × 4 = 32 + 2 = **34**

8 × 8 = 64/2 = 32 × 8 = 256 + 4 = **260**

16 × 16 = 256/2 = 124 × 16 = 1984 + 8 = **1992**

32 × 32 = 1024/2 = 512 × 32 = 16,384 + 16 = **16,400**

Preparation of 16-cell Magic Square (4 × 4)

Step One

Start with number 1 on the left corner top and place numbers serially on the 16 squares as shown below.

1			4
	6	7	
	10	11	
13			16

Step Two

The blank boxes should be filled from bottom boxes starting from 2. The numbers that are already filled in should be omitted. This can be done as follows:

	15	14	
12			9
8			5
	3	2	

Step Three (Final)

The final output is as follows:

The total is 34.

1	15	14	4
12	6	7	9
8	10	11	5
13	3	2	16

Preparation of 64-cell Magic Square (8 × 8)

First Step

1			4	5			8
	10	11			14	15	
	18	19			22	23	
25			28	29			32
33			36	37			40
	42	43			46	47	
	50	51			54	55	
57			60	61			64

Second Step

Fill all the blank boxes starting from 2 at the bottom and end with 63 at the top of the boxes next to 1.

	63	62			59	58	
56			53	52			49
48			45	44			41
	39	38			35	34	
	31	30			27	26	
24			21	20			17
16			13	12			9
	7	6			3	2	

Third Step (Final)

Combine both the numbers and prepare one square consisting of 64 cells.

The total is 260.

1	63	62	4	5	59	58	8
56	10	11	53	52	14	15	49
48	18	19	45	44	22	23	41
25	39	38	28	29	35	34	32
33	31	30	36	37	27	26	40
24	42	43	21	20	46	47	17
16	50	51	13	12	54	55	9
57	7	6	60	61	3	2	64

Following the same pattern you can now prepare 16 × 16 = 256 squares, 32 × 32 = 1,024 squares, or any number of squares starting with number 1.

Preparation of 256-cell Magic Square (16 × 16)

As per the explanations given previously, the 256-cell Magic Square is prepared as follows:
The total is 2056 – horizontally, vertically and diagonally.

1	255	254	4	5	251	250	8	9	247	246	12	13	243	242	16
240	18	19	237	236	22	23	233	232	26	27	229	228	30	31	225
224	34	35	221	220	38	39	217	216	42	43	213	212	46	47	209
49	207	206	52	53	203	202	56	57	199	198	60	61	195	194	64
65	191	190	68	69	187	186	72	73	183	182	76	77	179	178	80
176	82	83	173	172	86	87	169	168	90	91	165	164	94	95	161
160	98	99	157	156	102	103	153	152	106	107	149	148	110	111	145
113	143	142	116	117	139	138	120	121	135	134	124	125	131	130	128
129	127	126	132	133	123	122	136	137	119	118	140	141	115	114	144
112	146	147	109	108	150	151	105	104	154	155	101	100	158	159	97
96	162	163	93	92	166	167	89	88	170	171	85	84	174	175	81
177	79	78	180	181	75	74	184	185	71	70	188	189	67	66	192
193	63	62	196	197	59	58	200	201	55	54	204	205	51	50	208
48	210	211	45	44	214	215	41	40	218	219	37	36	222	223	33
32	226	227	29	28	230	231	25	24	234	235	21	20	238	239	17
241	15	14	244	245	11	10	248	249	7	6	252	253	3	2	256

Preparation of 16-cell Magic Square with any given number

Steps to be followed:

1. Find out the code for a 16-cell square. This can be computed as follows:

   4 × 4 = 16/2 = 8 – 1 = 7. Number 7 is the code.

2. If the chosen number is 98, divide this by 4, and we get 24 + 2. Deduct 7 from 24 = 17. Number 17 should be the starting number if we want to get a total of 98 in a 16-cell square.

The total is 98.

17	31	30	20
28	22	23	25
24	26	27	21
29	19	18	32

The same procedure should be followed for preparing 64-cell squares and 256-cell squares.

Preparation of 64-cell Square with any given number (8 × 8).

1. Find out the code for a 64-cell square (8 × 8). This is computed as follows: 8 × 8 = 64/2 = 32 – 1 = 31.
2. 31 is the code for a 64-cell square.
3. Let us take 372. This will be divisible by 8 plus 4. 372/8 = 46 + 4.
4. Deduct the code number 31 from 46 = 15.
5. 15 should be the starting number.
6. Accordingly, a 64-cell square is prepared as under:

The total is 372 – horizontally, vertically and diagonally.

15	77	76	18	19	73	72	22
70	24	25	67	66	28	29	63
62	32	33	59	58	36	37	55
39	53	52	42	43	49	48	46
47	45	44	50	51	41	40	54
38	56	57	35	34	60	61	31
30	64	65	27	26	68	69	23
71	21	20	74	75	17	16	78

Preparation of 36-cell Magic Square (6 × 6)

The minimum number that can be accommodated in a 36-cell square (6 × 6) is worked as follows:

6 × 6 = 36/2 = 18 × 6 = 108 + 3 = 111

I III

8	1	6	26	19	24
3	**5**	7	21	23	25
4	9	2	22	27	20
35	28	33	17	10	15
30	**32**	34	12	14	16
31	36	29	13	18	11

IV II

Note: In this you will find four 9-cell magic squares, which would work out to 36-cell magic squares. Fill the four blocks as done in a 9-cell square. First to be filled up is the left side top, the second one is the right side bottom, the third should be the right side top and the last one should be the left side bottom. In this way 36 numbers should be filled consecutively.

The next step is to interchange the following numbers: 8 and 35; 4 and 31; 5 and 32. These numbers are kept in bold letters. The final 36-cell magic square is prepared as follows. The total is 111.

35	1	6	26	19	24
3	**32**	7	21	23	25
31	9	2	22	27	20
8	28	33	17	10	15
30	**5**	34	12	14	16
4	36	29	13	18	11

Note: Interchanged numbers are indicated in bold letters.

Preparation of 36-cell Magic Square with any given number

1. Find out the code number for a 36-cell square. 6 × 6 = 36/2 = 18 – 1 = 17.
2. 17 is the code for a 36-cell square.
3. The number that can be accommodated should be above 111. This is the minimum number for a 36-cell square. Any number above 111 should be chosen.
4. The number that is chosen should be divisible by 6 plus 3.
5. Accordingly, let us take 153 as the chosen number. If we divide 153 by 6 we get a quotient of 25 and the remainder is 3. Therefore, this number can be accommodated in a 36-cell square.
6. Deduct the code number 17 from 25. The result is 8, which should be the starting number to prepare a 36-cell square to accommodate the number 153.
7. The magic square is prepared as follows:

First Magic Square

15	8	13	33	26	31
10	**12**	14	28	30	32
11	16	9	29	34	27
42	35	40	24	17	22
37	**39**	41	19	21	23
38	43	36	20	25	18

The following numbers are to be interchanged: 15 and 42; 11 and 38; 12 and 39. The final magic square is prepared as follows:

Final Magic Square – the total is 153.

42	8	13	33	26	31
10	**39**	14	28	30	32
38	16	9	29	34	27
15	35	40	24	17	22
37	**12**	41	19	21	23
11	43	36	20	25	18

Preparation of 100-cell Magic Square (10×10)

First Magic Square

I III

23	**6**	19	2	15	**73**	56	69	52	65
10	**18**	**1**	14	22	60	**68**	51	64	72
17	5	**13**	**21**	9	67	55	**63**	71	59
4	**12**	**25**	8	16	54	**62**	75	58	66
11	**24**	7	20	3	**61**	74	57	70	53
98	**81**	94	77	90	**48**	31	44	27	40
85	**93**	**76**	89	97	35	**43**	26	39	47
92	80	**88**	**96**	84	42	30	**38**	46	34
79	**87**	**100**	83	91	29	**37**	50	33	41
86	**99**	82	95	78	**36**	49	32	45	28

IV II

Note: There are four 25-cell magic squares. Fill the four blocks as done in a 25-cell square.

The numbers given in bold should be interchanged as shown below:

23 and 98 / 11 and 86 / 6 and 81 / 18 and 93 / 12 and 87 / 24 and 99 / 1 and 76 / 13 and 88 / 25 and 100 / 21 and 96 / 73 and 48 / 61 and 36 / 68 and 43 / 62 and 37 / 63 and 38.

The second magic square is prepared based on the changes referred to above.

98	81	19	2	15	48	56	69	52	65
10	93	76	14	22	60	43	51	64	72
17	5	**88**	96	9	67	55	**38**	71	59
4	87	100	8	16	54	37	75	58	66
86	99	**7**	20	3	36	74	**57**	70	53
23	6	94	77	90	73	31	44	27	40
85	18	1	89	97	35	68	26	39	47
92	80	13	21	84	42	30	63	46	34
79	12	25	83	91	29	62	50	33	41
11	24	82	95	78	61	49	32	45	28

The final 100-cell magic square is prepared by adjusting the numbers that are kept in bold in the second square. The numbers to be interchanged are **88 and 38**, and **7 and 57**.

The total is 505 – horizontally, vertically and diagonally.

Final 100-cell Magic Square (10 × 10)

98	81	19	2	15	48	56	69	52	65
11	93	76	14	22	60	43	51	64	72
17	5	**38**	96	9	67	55	**88**	71	59
4	87	100	8	16	54	37	75	58	66
86	99	**57**	20	3	36	74	**7**	70	53
23	6	94	77	90	73	31	44	27	40
85	18	1	89	97	35	68	26	39	47
92	80	13	21	84	42	30	63	46	34
79	12	25	83	91	29	62	50	33	41
11	24	82	95	78	61	49	32	45	28

Preparation of 100-cell Magic Square with any given number.

1. Find out the code number for a 100-cell square.
2. This is computed as follows: 10 × 10 = 100/2 = 50 – 1 = 49.
3. Number 49 is the code for a 100-cell square.
4. The number that can be accommodated should be above 505 and divisible by 10 plus 5.
5. Accordingly, let us take number 905. If we divide 905 by 10 the quotient is 90 and the balance is 5.
6. To find out the starting number, deduct 49 from 90 = 41.
7. Number 41 should be the starting number for a total of 905 in a 100-cell magic square.
8. Based on the explanations given above, a 100-cell magic square is constructed to get a total of 905.

First Square

63	**46**	59	42	55	**113**	96	109	92	105
50	**58**	**41**	54	62	100	**108**	91	104	112
57	45	**53**	**61**	49	107	95	**103**	111	99
44	**52**	**65**	48	56	94	**102**	115	98	106
51	**64**	47	60	43	**101**	114	97	110	93
138	**121**	134	117	130	**88**	71	84	67	80
125	**133**	**116**	129	137	75	**83**	66	79	87
132	120	**128**	**136**	124	82	70	**78**	86	74
119	**127**	**140**	123	131	69	**77**	90	73	81
126	**139**	122	135	118	**76**	89	72	85	68

Second Square

138	121	59	42	55	88	96	109	92	105
50	133	116	54	62	100	83	91	104	112
57	45	**128**	136	49	107	95	**78**	111	99
44	127	140	48	56	94	77	115	98	106
126	139	**47**	60	43	76	114	**97**	110	93
63	46	134	117	130	113	71	84	67	80
125	58	41	129	137	75	108	66	79	87
132	120	53	61	124	82	70	103	86	74
119	52	65	123	131	69	102	90	73	81
51	64	122	135	118	101	89	72	85	68

Final Square

The total is 905 – horizontally, vertically and diagonally.

138	121	59	42	55	88	96	109	92	105
50	133	116	54	62	100	83	91	104	112
57	45	78	136	49	107	95	128	111	99
44	127	140	48	56	94	77	115	98	106
126	139	97	60	43	76	114	47	110	93
63	46	134	117	130	113	71	84	67	80
125	58	41	129	137	75	108	66	79	87
132	120	53	61	124	82	70	103	86	74
119	52	65	123	131	69	102	90	73	81
51	64	122	135	118	101	89	72	85	68

Some Unique Magic Squares

Here is a 16-cell magic square, innovated by Manadev, a Jain poet. The magic constant of this square is 34. This figure can be obtained horizontally, vertically, diagonally and also from various angles in 34 different ways.

5	16	3	10
4	9	6	15
14	7	12	1
11	2	13	8

The various combinations are shown below:

(1)	1	4	14	15	=	34	(19)	3	6	9	16	=	34
(2)	1	6	11	16	=	34	(20)	3	6	10	15	=	34
(3)	1	6	12	15	=	34	(21)	3	6	12	13	=	34
(4)	1	7	10	16	=	34	(22)	3	8	9	14	=	34
(5)	1	7	12	14	=	34	(23)	3	8	10	13	=	34
(6)	1	8	10	15	=	34	(24)	4	5	9	16	=	34
(7)	1	8	11	14	=	34	(25)	4	5	10	15	=	34
(8)	1	8	12	13	=	34	(26)	4	5	11	14	=	34
(9)	2	3	13	16	=	34	(27)	4	6	9	15	=	34
(10)	2	5	11	16	=	34	(28)	4	6	11	13	=	34
(11)	2	5	12	15	=	34	(29)	4	7	9	14		34
(12)	2	7	9	16	=	34	(30)	4	7	10	13	=	34
(13)	2	7	11	14	=	34	(31)	5	8	9	12	=	34
(14)	2	7	12	13	=	34	(32)	5	8	10	11	=	34
(15)	2	8	9	15	=	34	(33)	6	7	9	12	=	34
(16)	2	8	11	13	=	34	(34)	6	7	10	11	=	34
(17)	3	5	10	16	=	34							
(18)	3	5	12	14	=	34							

Akshaya Chakra

This is one of the most fascinating 16-cell magic squares. This has two unique features:

(1) The constant magic number of 34 can also be derived from 34 different angles.

(2) Any number above 34 can be accommodated in a 16-cell magic square based on this pattern. **This is called Akshaya Chakra because you can fill this square with any number of your choice, even numbers as well as odd numbers.**

9	6	3	16
4	15	10	5
14	1	8	11
7	12	13	2

Various combinations are shown in the following table:

(1)	1	4	13	16	=	34	(19)	3	5	12	14	=	34
(2)	1	4	14	15	=	34	(20)	3	6	9	16	=	34
(3)	1	6	11	16	=	34	(21)	3	6	10	15	=	34
(4)	1	6	12	15	=	34	(22)	3	6	12	13	=	34
(5)	1	7	10	16	=	34	(23)	3	8	9	14	=	34
(6)	1	7	12	14	=	34	(24)	3	8	10	13	=	34
(7)	1	8	10	15	=	34	(25)	4	5	9	16	=	34
(8)	1	8	11	14	=	34	(26)	4	5	10	15	=	34
(9)	1	8	12	13	=	34	(27)	4	5	11	14	=	34
(10)	2	3	13	16	=	34	(28)	4	6	9	15	=	34
(11)	2	3	14	15	=	34	(29)	4	7	9	14	=	34
(12)	2	5	11	16	=	34	(30)	4	7	10	13	=	34
(13)	2	5	12	15	=	34	(31)	5	8	9	12	=	34
(14)	2	7	9	16	=	34	(32)	5	8	10	11	=	34
(15)	2	7	11	14	=	34	(33)	6	7	9	12	=	34
(16)	2	7	12	13	=	34	(34)	6	7	10	11	=	34
(17)	2	8	11	13	=	34							
(18)	3	5	10	16	=	34							

This 16-cell magic square can be transformed into another magic square, which can accommodate any number above 34. This can be verified as follows:

Choose any number. Let us take 91. This number should be accommodated in the magic square as per the following procedure:

91 – 34 = 57/4 = 14 is the quotient and 1 is the remainder. Based on the magic square given above, add the quotient (14) and the remainder (1) with the highest numbers in the magic squares, i.e. 13, 14, 15, 16. (13 + 15 = 28, 14 + 15 = 29, 15 + 15 = 30, 16 + 15 = 31). Add the quotient 14 to the remaining numbers starting from 1 to 12. The new magic square will be as follows:

The total is 91.

23	20	17	31
18	30	24	19
29	15	22	25
21	26	28	16

Say the chosen number is 35. After deducting 34, we get a balance of 1. This number should be added to the highest four numbers mentioned above. The new magic square can be prepared as follows:

The total is 35.

9	6	3	17
4	16	10	5
15	1	8	11
7	12	14	2

Significance of Akshaya Chakra

This magic square has been kept a secret by those who believed that this magic square would bring luck and good fortune to those possessing it. In the past, and even today, people would engrave this magic square in silver and golden plates and keep it with them at all times.

To boost your brainpower choose any number at random and try to accommodate it in this magic square. Not only will this give you good luck but your brain will be stimulated to a considerable extent.

✡✡✡

Appendix A

Availability of Supplements mentioned in this book:

S. No	Supplements	Brand	Company	Form	Unit	Price
1.	Gingko Biloba	Ginkocer	Ranbaxy	Tablet	10	Rs.84
2.	Ginseng	Revital	Ranbaxy	Capsule	10	Rs.61
3.	Vitamin E	Evion	Merck	Capsule 400 IU	10	Rs.23
4.	Vitamin B1, B3, B6, B12, Vitamin C and E, Calcium, Magnesium, Zinc, Multi-vitamin, Multi-mineral	Becadexamin	Glaxo	Capsule	30	Rs.25
5.	Vitamin C and E Zinc Selenium	Selace I	Universal Medicare	Capsule	15	Rs.96
6.	Gingko Biloba, Ginseng, Garlic	GGG-24	Mona Pharma (Sali)	Capsule	10	Rs.74

Index

✡✡✡

Bibliography

AL KORAN, ***How to use the Hidden Power of Your Mind*** – Coles Publishing Company Ltd, Toronto, 1980

ALAN BADDELEY, ***Your Memory – A User's Guide*** – Rupa & Co., Delhi, 2000

ALFRED JOHN, ***IQ for All*** – Goodwill Publishing House, New Delhi

ALLEN F. HARRISON, ***The Art of Thinking*** – Barkley Books, 1982

ANDREW WRIGHT, ***Improve Your Mind*** – Cambridge University Press, New York, 1987

ANGELA BOOTH, ***Improve Your Memory in 21 Days*** – Prentice Hall, 1997

BARBARA B. BROWN, ***Super Mind*** – Bantam Books, 1998

BARNARD D.P., ***Brain Twisters*** – Gaurav Publishing House

BARRY R. CLARKE, ***Puzzles for Pleasure*** – Cambridge University Press, 1994

BEDI C.S., ***You and Your Intelligence*** – Kalyani Publishers, 1974

BERNIE ZILBERGELD & ARNOLD A. LAZARUS, ***Mind Power*** – Ivy Books, 1991

BOBBI DEPORTER & MIKEHERNACKI, ***Quantum Learning*** – Piatkus, London, 1992

BRIAN CLEGG, **Instant Brainpower** – Kogan Page, 2000

BRIAN LANCASTER, ***Mind, Brain and Human Potential*** – Element, New York, 1991

CHARLES BARRY TOWNSEND, ***World's Best Puzzles*** – Orient Paperbacks, 1997

CHARLES BARRY TOWNSEND, ***World's Toughest Puzzles*** – Orient Paperbacks, 2000

CHITTARANJAN ANDRADE, ***Riddles for all Ages*** – Pauline Publications, 1996

CORINNE JACKER, ***Men, Memory and Machine*** – Dell, New York, 1966

CYNTHIA R. GREEN, ***Total Memory Workout*** – Bantam Books, 2001

DANIELLE C. LAPP, ***Maximizing Your Memory Power*** – Barron's Educational Series

DANDEKAR W.N., ***Fundamentals of Educational Psychology*** -- Moghe Prakashan, 1970

DARRYL FRANCIS, ***Puzzles and Teasers for Everyone*** – Gaurav Publishing House

DAVID MOXON, ***Memory*** – Heinemann, 2000

DENIS POSTLE, ***The Mind Gymnasium*** – McGraw-Hill, New York, 1988

DENIS WATTLEY, ***Empires of the Mind*** – Allen & Unwin

DHARMA SINGH KHALSA, ***Mind Miracle (Brain Longevity)*** – Random House, London, 1999

DIANA BEAVER, ***Lazy Learning*** – Element, Rockport, 1994

DOMINIC O'BRIEN, ***Learn to Remember*** – Duncan Baird Publishers, 2000

DONALD I. PEAKE, ***Mindflow*** – D.B. Taraporavala, 1983

EDWARD DE BONO, ***The Mechanism of Mind*** – Penguin Books, 1969

EUSTACE CHESSER, ***Know Yourself*** – Gorgi Books, 1965

EYSENCK H.J., ***Know Your Own IQ*** – Penguin Books, 1973

GEOFFREY BUDWORTH, ***The Right Way to Improve Your Memory*** – Jaico Publishing House, 1995

GELLIAN BUTLER & TONY HOPE, ***Manage Your Mind*** – Oxford University Press, 1995

GEORGE J. SUMMERS, ***The Great Book of Puzzles and Teasers*** – Jaico, 1986

GILLES AZZOPARDI, ***Simple Methods for Measuring Your IQ*** – Infinity Books, 2001

GOPALAKRISHNAN, ***Mental Health and You*** – India Book House, 1986

GOPI KRISHNA, ***The Wonders of the Brain*** – UBS Publishers, 1993

GUPTA M.K., ***How to Control Mind and be Stress Free*** – Pustak Mahal, 1998

HANS RAJ BHATIA, ***Making the Most of Your Mind*** – Pearl Publications, 1969

HAROLD SHERMAN, ***Know Your Own Mind*** – Fawcett, 1971

HARRY LORAYNE, ***Super Power Memory*** – Fell Publishers, 1990

HARRY LORAYNE & JERRY LUCAS, ***The Memory Book***

IRVING JACOBSON, ***The Power of Your Mind*** – Vikas, 1975

JACE, ***Standard Quiz Book*** – Goodwill Publishing House, Delhi

JACK BLACK, ***Mindstore for Personal Development*** – Thorson, 1996

JACQUELINE DINEEN, ***Remembering Made Easy*** – Jaico, 1977

JEAN MARIE STINE, ***Double Your Brain Power*** – Prentice Hall, 1977

JEAN CARPER, ***Your Miracle Brain*** – Quill, 2001

JEFF BUDWORTH, ***Tapping Your Hidden Memory Power*** – Bob Adams, 1991

JIM SUKACH, ***Challenging Puzzles*** – Orient Paperbacks, 1997

JOAD, C.E.M., ***How Our Mind Works*** – Westhouse, 1946

JOAN MINNINGER & ELEANOR DUGAN, ***Make Your Mind Work for You*** – Pocket Books, 1988

JOHN D'SILVA, ***Check Your Own IQ*** – Kiran

JOHN JAMES, ***Quiz & Puzzles*** – 1, 2, 3 & 4, Gaurav Publishers

JOHN R. BEWS, ***How to Use Your Brain*** – Jaico, 1997

JOLENE ANDERSON, ***Miracle Mind – Secrets of the Ancients*** – Taraporavala, 1983

JOSE SILVA & BURT GOLDMAN, ***Silva Mind Control Method*** – Pocket Books, 1988

JOSEPH MURPHY, ***The Miracles of Mind Dynamics*** – Prentice Hall, 1964

JOSEPH MURPHY, ***The Amazing Laws of Cosmic Mind Power*** – Parker Publishing Company, 1965

JOYCE WYCOFF, ***Mind Mapping*** – Barkley Books, 1991

KAMLESH MAHINDRA, ***Brain Teasers*** – Sterling Paperbacks

KARL ALBRECHT, ***Brain Power*** – Simon & Schuster, 1992

KEITH HARRY & PAMELA WEINTRAUB, ***Right Brain Learning in 30 Days*** – Aquarian/Thorson, 1992

KEN RUSSELL & PHILIP CARTER, ***Testing Your IQ,*** Infinity Books

KENNETH GIUFRE & THERESA FOY DIGERONIMO, ***The Care and Feeding of Your Brain*** – East-West Books, 2000

KEVIN PAUL, ***Study Smarter, Not Harder*** – Jaico, 2000

LAWRENCE C. KATZ & MANNING RUBIN, ***Keep Your Brain Alive***

LINDA VERLEE WILLIAMS, ***Teaching for the Two-sided*** – Touchstone, 1986

LUIS S.R. VAS, ***Dynamics of Mind Management*** – Jaico, 1991

LOUISE SYNDER JOHNSON, ***Know Your Mind*** – Crest Publishing House, 2000

MANOJ ANAND, ***How to Improve Your Memory***

MARGARET O. HYDE, ***Mind Drugs***, Jeeth Publications

MARILYN VOSSAVANT & LEONORE, ***Brain Power***, India Book Distributors, 1992

MARY COLLINS & JAMES DROVER, ***Experimental Psychology***, Lyall, 1968

MATT OECHSLI, ***Mind Power for Students*** – Magna Publishing Co., 2000

MAXWELL MALTZ, ***Psycho Cybernetics*** – Wiltshire, 1960

MELVIN POWERS, ***Dynamic Thinking*** – St Paul, 1955

MICHAEL D. CHAFETZ, ***How to Improve Your Brainpower at any Age***, 1992

MICHAEL HUTCHISON, ***Mega Brain*** – Ballantine Books, 1991

MICHAEL HUTCHISON, ***Mega Brain Power*** – Hyperion, 1994

MITRA A.K., ***Improve Your Memory and Mental Power*** – Pankaj Publication, 1978

MURTHY K.R.K., ***Mathemagic*** – Janapada Prakashana

NORMAN D. WILLIS, ***Tricky Logic Puzzles*** – Orient Paperbacks, 1995

OSHO, ***The Cessation of the Mind*** – Diamond Books, 1996

PAUL J. LEIGHTON, ***Delta Mind Dynamics*** – Prentice Hall, 1980

PAUL SLOANE & DES MACHALE, ***Super Lateral Thinking Puzzles*** – Sterling Publishing, New York, 2000

PEKELIS V., ***Realise Your Potential*** – Mir Publishers, 1987

PETER TOON, PENNY TRIP & MARK EVANS, ***Your Mind*** – Harrap Publishing House, 1990

PILLAI C.S., ***Know Your Mind*** – Vedanta Publications

POTTER & SEBASTIAN ORFALI, ***Brain Boosters*** – Rohin Publishers, 1993

PRISCILLA DONOVAN & JACQUELYN WONDER, ***The Forever Mind*** – William Morrow & Co., 1994

RAMESH B.G., ***Mathematics Quiz*** – M/s Narayana Iyenger, 1998

RAMESH B.G., ***Amazing Puzzles*** – M/s Narayana Iyengar, 1999

RAVI NARULA, ***Brain Teasers*** – Jaico, 2002

READER'S DIGEST, ***ABCs of the Human Mind*** – 1990

RICHARD PALMER & CHRIS POPE, ***Brain Train*** – E & FN Spon, 1992

RICHARD LAWRENCE, ***Journey into Supermind*** – Souvenir Press, 1995

RICHARD LEVITON, ***Brain Builders*** – Prentice Hall, 1995

RITA CARTER, ***Mapping the Mind*** – Seven Dials, 1998

ROBERT WINSTON, **The Human Mind** – Bantam Press, 2003

ROGER B. YEPSEN, ***How to Boost Your Brain Power*** – HarperCollins, 1992

ROGER VON OECH, ***A Whack on the Side of the Head*** – Indus, 1993

ROY MASTERS, ***How Your Mind Can Keep You Well*** – Better Yourself Books, 1998

SAM PHILIPS, ***21 Tips for a Super Power Memory*** – Goodwill Publishing House

SHEILA OSTRANDER, LYNN SCHROEDER & NANCY OSTRANDER, ***Super Learning 2000*** – Delacorte Press, 1994

SWAMY BUDHANANDA, ***The Mind and Its Control*** – Advaidha Ashrama, 1992

TANUSHREE PODDER, ***Smart Memory*** – Pustak Mahal, 2002

TERRY H. STICKLES, ***Mind Stretching Puzzles*** – Orient Paperbacks, 2001

THEODOR LAURENCE, ***Helping Yourself with Psycho-symbology*** – Taraporavala, 1990

THOMAS ARMSTRONG, ***Developing Your Many Intelligences*** – Plume, 1993

TOM WUJEC, ***Mental Fitness: Exercises to Improve Your Brainpower*** – Orient Paperbacks, 1991

TONY BUZON, ***Make the Most of Your Mind*** – Pan Books, 1977

VERNON MARK, ***Brain Power*** – Houghton Miffin Company, 1999

WILLIAM H. CALVIN, ***How Brains Think*** – 1996

WILLIAM BERNARD & JULES LEOPOLD, ***Test Yourself*** – Gorgi Books, 1972

✡✡✡

Books on

Self-Improvement

₹80/-

100 Lessons to live life Blooming

₹180/-

₹120/-

₹80/-

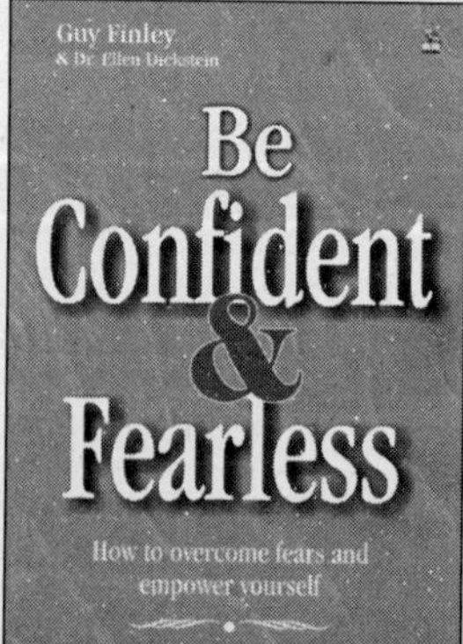

₹140/-

Books on

Self-Improvement

GREAT IDEAS THAT WILL KEEP YOU STRESS-FREE & RELAXED AT WORK

PRATIK P. SURANA

₹195/-

Er. M.K. Gupta

How to Remain Ever Happy

Over 125 tips

Release stress & anxiety and live life with joy & happiness

₹150/-

77 LESSONS to remain EVER POSITIVE

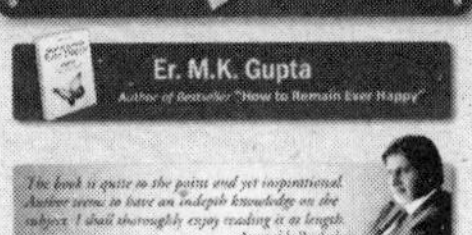

₹120/-

BACK TO SCHOOL @30

Handling Midlife Crises

by

Being Righteous again
Being Disciplined again
Being Obedient again
Being Honest in Relationships again

Rashmi Singh

₹150/-

365 Recipes That will make you Think Positive

Bestselling author of *I Had It All the Time* & *The Dragon Doesn't Live here Anymore*
Co-Writer of *Chicken Soup for the Soul*

ALAN COHEN

₹195/-

Live Life Worthwhile

70 Ways to Enjoy it

70 Lessons along with Anecdotes and Bits of Wit that Inspire and Motivate you for a TRULY FULFILLING LIFE

Murli Chari

₹195/-